The Golden Thread

The Golden Thread

Diary of Mrs. Elsie Koll
Missionary to China

Overcomer Press, Inc.
Publishers
Owosso, Michigan

Published by
Overcomer Press, Inc.
310 West Main Street
P.O. Box 70
Owosso, Michigan 48867
U.S.A.

Copyright © 1982, The Estate of Elsie Koll

All rights reserved. Apart from the
purpose of private study, research or review,
no part of this book may be reproduced
by any process without the prior
permission of Overcomer Press, Inc.

Library of Congress Catalog Card Number: 81-86332
ISBN: 0-942504-00-3

Printed and bound in the
United States of America

Photoset in Paladium by The Type-Righters, Owosso, Michigan
Printed by Thomson-Shore, Inc., Dexter, Michigan

Editor's Foreword

The story about to be told has its major setting in China. The Christian mission work it describes is that associated with those known as brethren.

This work commenced in 1904 when Thomas Hutton of England opened a mission in the city of Hinghwa, Kiangsu province. His daughter, Annie, and Miss C. H. von Poseck (the hymnwriter) joined him, together with evangelist Heinrich Ruck of Germany who made a new translation of the New Testament and a Chinese hymnbook later used in the assemblies there. He married Annie Hutton.

Other missionaries followed: Gustav and Lili Koll of Germany; Wilhelm and Elsie Koll of Germany and England respectively; Dr. and Mrs. Hans Neuffer of Germany (the doctor being a skilled surgeon and Bible teacher); Ruth Neuffer (Dr. Neuffer's sister); Misses Thorens and Junod of Switzerland and Miss Verkijk, amongst several others. A hospital and school was established and the missionary work branched out into the cities of Kwangping Hsien, Kwangping Fu, Peking, where a bookshop was established, Nanking, Chinkiang and various rural villages such as Poh Chu.

When the Communists took over after the Second World War, there were assemblies in seven cities and many Chinese brethren. Foreign missionaries were soon forced to leave and have not returned.

There is no reliable information available today as to the present condition and extent of the faithful mission work Elsie Koll and her husband had to leave behind in 1946. But the Lord Himself knows and that is what counts in eternity.

Contents

Illustrations

Authoress's Preface

This little book is not intended to be about missionary work or the preparation for it, much less is it intended to be about Elsie Koll; rather is it a record of the way in which events, small as well as great, in a Christian life, follow the pattern of God's gracious intent for that life. To this extent it has been necessary to cover a wide field of preparation and subsequent work and to lift the theme out of the realm of hypothesis. An actual case history is quoted, necessarily my own.

Many young people seek 'God's guidance' for their lives and if these pages help some to take notice of an ordering of thoughts and circumstances by His (often unseen) power, their object will have been achieved.

May all the glory be seen to belong to God Himself who may see fit to bless and encourage the reader as the seeming little and unimportant events of life are appreciated because allowed, and indeed often arranged, by the One 'whose we are and whom we serve'.

Introduction

Veteran missionary Elsie Koll was called by her Lord to higher service on October 1st, 1977 in her 81st year. She died 'in harness' as a good soldier of Jesus Christ — having become unwell while interpreting at the 1977 Zurich Conference.

To those who knew her she was held in high esteem and affection. She had the gift of being able to combine the life of a pioneer missionary wife with that of being a devoted mother to her children.

For about thirty years Elsie Koll worked devotedly beside her husband Wilhelm, in China. The numerous experiences she had of passing through countless troubles and dangers made her the godly, intelligent and intensely practical woman she was.

Although she retired from missionary work in China, she never retired from active service for her Master. She devoted herself 'at home' and on the Continent to activities among women and children, translation work, and interpreting for many years at the annual Zurich Conference.

The writer of this introduction knew Elsie Koll for the last 25 years of her life. Having himself been engaged in missionary work, it was always a real challenge and spiritual inspiration to visit with her. Even now the memory of her, to all of us, is still fresh and precious.

May this book be a true inspiration to all who read it. May it stir us up to take the 'torch' from her hands as we seek to imitate her faith.

Ipswich, 1981   *Cor Bruins*

Chapter 1

Prayer and a Promise

L ife for me began, and nearly ended, in one of the two rooms of our home in a quiet, terraced house typical of middle-class London in 1897. The first strand of a Golden Thread in an otherwise ordinary life made its appearance one day when a sad little group gathered in the living room to console a weeping mother. Her third child, a little girl of seven months, lay apparently dying in the adjacent bedroom. No luxury or elaborate decor cushioned the broken-hearted parents against what seemed disaster, as they had already lost a little girl at birth, then a son at seven months. Now it would seem this precious daughter was to leave them; but love and prayer turned those two rooms into a happy home and a sanctuary.

Father, kneeling at the cot-side, prayed and was moved to say that if God could spare him this child she should be set apart for Him. That prayer was heard by the Father in heaven who had given His only begotten Son for them. The request was in line with His plan for the precarious life; for the child who that day 'took a turn for the better' has been spared beyond the span of 'three score years and ten' to write these words today.

I did not hear the story of Father's prayer until twenty

years later, after I had already answered the call of God
to the mission field in China. By then the Golden Thread
of God's ordering was forming links in a chain in His
plan for my life. Surely this is what the Psalmist had in
mind when he wrote 'Thine eyes did see my substance,
yet being unperfect.'

Red Card for Danger

Babyhood passed quickly and normally into an aware-
ness at an early age that life held treasures to be
explored. In school at five years old I had already an
insatiable thirst for knowledge and an ambition to be at
the top, which replaced any inclination to play about.
But my passion for reading was halted abruptly at the
age of eight when the visiting eye-specialist at school
gave me a red card urging immediate attendance at
Moorfields Eye Hospital. As we journeyed home in the
horse-drawn bus, I noticed my mother quietly shedding
tears and in answer to my whispered question she said,
'They scolded me at the hospital for not taking earlier
precautions and they fear you may go blind.' With
childlike abandon I was not impressed by the seriousness
of the situation but rather began practising all kinds of
activities with my eyes closed, 'just in case . . . '
    Again my parents resorted to special prayer and
decided that we should consult a Christian friend at
Leicester who was also an optician. I well recollect the
journey by train with my father but did not know that
here the Golden Thread was spinning again, unseen this
time by us, for the significance of this visit did not
appear until long after the event. For me at the time it
was just a great adventure comprising a train journey
from Marylebone Station, making new friends and
having a pair of spectacles!

Swinging Under a Lilac Tree

Two years packed with happy days at home and school

bring us to another glimpse of the Golden Thread; years filled with memories of my father, 'the singing man' as the neighbours called him, as he entered into his children's play (for by this time I had twin sisters), took us out every holiday and gave us a trip to the seaside in the summer. This trip started at the street-door for, Father being a saddler with connections, we always had a horse-cab to the railway station. Above all, and providing the background to these joyous activities, there was the atmosphere of peace and security of our home where God's Word had the first place and on our knees was found the solution to problems.

At the age of ten came the opportunity to sit for the Junior County Scholarship which could provide entrance to the High School. To this day I remember the question set for English Composition, 'What do you do on Saturday mornings, and what would you like to do?' My answer told of all the chores we were expected to do in turns at home — knife cleaning, silver polishing, dusting and so on; then in one short paragraph my wish that I might sit in a swing under a flowering lilac tree, with a book to read and an apple to eat! How this had catered for my physical and mental needs in one sentence I did not realise at the time, but it won me the scholarship.

Then came the snag, when one had to 'pass the doctor.' Eyes again loomed large. Insistence by the doctor upon specialist treatment was followed by a list of four specialists of which I must choose one to attend to my eyes. At breakfast the next morning we knelt as Father asked God to guide us to select the right one as we knew none of them. The list was sent to our Christian optician friend who replied that the only one he knew personally was 'the lady doctor.' A woman specialist was a real exception in those Edwardian days but Father took the information as an answer to prayer — and the Golden Thread made another secure loop, as will emerge later

in the story. She was found to be a dear Christian and
each subsequent yearly visit had the additional blessing
of fellowship over the Word of God.

Belief — Fear — Victory

Two more years — and at twelve for me came the most
important decision a human being is ever called to take;
the yielding of the heart to the Lord Jesus. I do not know
when I was born again, but the confession was made
one morning after Mother had opened a letter from
Grandfather in which he wrote,'What would happen to
Elsie if the Lord Jesus were to come today?' My response
was immediate, 'I should go to be with those caught up
because He is my Saviour.'

From then on, however, came the realisation of how
far I was from Christian living, but then came into my
life two very important people — shall we say skilled
weavers of Golden Thread? One was my Sunday school
teacher, Miss Keene, and the other her friend, Miss Cole
(afterwards Mrs. Maxwell Smith), who held a Bible
Class on Saturday evenings. To these dear souls I could,
and did, go with all my fears — and I had some fears,
for as I read the Word of God for myself, John Chapter
15 terrified me lest I should be an unfruitful branch to be
cast out. Also Hebrews 10 worried me lest I should have
sinned wilfully and so have trodden underfoot the Son
of God. Patient instruction showed me that the very fact
of my anxiety about these things was proof of the Holy
Spirit working in me; that I was born again, never to
perish, with a growing desire to live more like Jesus.

One of my besetting sins was to 'answer back' my
mother who was a quiet, godly woman, though no
logical thinker, and easy to beat in argument. One
Saturday evening at Bible Class my sin was revealed to
me and I knew that I must apologise to Mother. Never
had the homeward walk taken so long and when upon
arrival I was told there were visitors the devil quickly

suggested, 'You need not do it tonight.' But the Lord whispered otherwise. He won and I went up at once and told Mother I was sorry. I record this because it was a great milestone on my way to overcoming that fault. After all, the Golden Thread has to have anchorage.

Chapter 2

Saddlery to Grocery

School with its wonderful opportunities for study continued to be a joy to me but at the age of 15 a family crisis came which threatened to alter the whole course of my life if God had not been working out the plan for the work He had prepared for me.

Father was a saddler making harness for the horses which pulled hansom-cabs and had gradually built up a nice business with several employees, but when the new taxi-cab began to travel the London streets, business slowly but surely declined until family finances were very low indeed. One Saturday he said to Mother, when he was due to go up to the Midlands to conduct some meetings, 'Dare I spend the last sovereign on the fare?' Up to this point he had felt like Elijah at the brook Cherith, for although he had seen the water drying up day by day, he always believed that God had somewhere commanded the 'widow woman' to sustain him. So in faith he set off for the station.

On the way he met an old acquaintance of the saddlery trade, who worked for the London General Omnibus Company making harness for the horses which drew the buses. This man's wife and daughter kept a small general shop in our neighbourhood. As

they spoke that morning and he asked about the
business, guessing that things were not too flourishing,
he presently said to Father, 'Why not buy our little shop?
We want to retire.' Immediately my father had the
feeling that here lay some guidance about his need, but
replied, 'Yes, I would like to start again but I have no
ready cash, only some property.' 'I am afraid that will
not do,' said the other, 'I must have cash so I must try to
sell elsewhere.'

Now the old man was an unbeliever and a strong
whiskey drinker but Father told him to try to sell for
cash as he was confident that if God meant him to have
the business, he would find he could not. Some months
passed and the brook was nearly dried up when one day
the would-be vendor came to Father, cursing and
saying, 'I don't know what you have done but I cannot
seem to sell, so I will take the property instead!' Then all
our lives were suddenly turned topsyturvy. Before we
realised it we owned a shop and were selling cooked
meats, groceries and confectionery without any training
or the least idea of how it should be done. All the hams
(in summer about forty per week) were cooked on the
premises and in those days of no pre-packaging, one
had to weigh and pack everything down to half an
ounce of pepper. Great blocks of salt had to be sawn up
into pennyworths, huge cheeses cut with a wire and
ham and bacon carved by hand.

Deviation to a Degree

At this point the turn of events looked like diverting the
whole course of my life. Father said that he could not
employ labour before he had himself grasped the trade,
so I must leave school to help since my twin sisters were
not yet fourteen years old, the school leaving age. In
truth I was a little weary of the piles of homework in
preparation for matriculation examinations and the
thrill of learning something new had its normal appeal

for a teenager. But a watchful heavenly Father ordered another stitch of the Golden Thread and when Father wrote to my headmistress explaining why I must leave school and give up my scholarship, she paid him a visit. She begged him not to take me away at that juncture and promised I should be excused all afternoon activities, needlework, art and the like, and that homework should be reduced to a minimum, as I was quite ready for the examination which could not, in any case, be taken until I was sixteen years old.

So began my new life, school from 9 a.m. to 1 p.m., serving and working in the shop from 2 p.m. to 11 p.m. (midnight on Saturdays, since there were no early closing regulations in those days). The teachers at school had orders to let me sleep if I dozed off in lesson time, as I sometimes did. This life continued until my sisters, who did not wish to study, could leave school. I called this time my prison years because I could not go out to meetings except on Sundays, but the Lord sustained all the way.

Meanwhile the Golden Thread was being woven another stitch without my knowledge at school. The science mistress wanted me to take chemistry as a subject in matriculation, whereas the language teacher wanted me to take German. My own feelings were neutral since one could take a degree in mathematics in the arts or science. The One directing my life, however, led victory for the German teacher and I took German as well as French and Latin in the examination the following year. How much I should need German later, was hidden from my eyes for many years. After my sisters took over in the shop, study for me prevailed again. Upon matriculation I was offered an extra scholarship year so that four of the subjects required for Intermediate (A level) were passed before entering University. This meant four years in University, three years for an Honour's degree in pure and applied

mathematics, and one year in teacher training. In order
to catch up with some of the subjects needed for the
latter, I attended Training College on a Wednesday and
Saturday, and during the long vacation, did three weeks
of school teaching practice each year.

Eyes Up and Eyes Right

Although by this time qualified as far as the studies were
concerned, I now faced the inevitable medical
examination. How vividly still remains the mental
picture of that cubicle where we prepared for the usual
tests of heart and lungs, then emerging at last to hear the
decision of two doctors. Their faces were grave as I
approached and I must confess my heart sank. At last
one spoke, 'We are fully satisfied with all the tests
except the vision. It is doubtful whether your eyes
would stand the long years of study.' What could I say?
My whole career hung on their decision. Then the
second doctor asked, 'Which specialist looks after your
eyes?' and when I named the lady doctor chosen by my
parents many years earlier, he exclaimed, 'Oh, if Dr.
Leney has charge of her eyes, I think we could pass her
on the strength of her right eye.'

Never had the Golden Thread shone with greater
brilliance. My eyes were lifted to Him, higher than the
hills, from whence had indeed come 'my strength.' My
heart lifted in praise to God for His guidance to my
parents in the days when I could have done nothing
about it.

Chapter 3

Belief in
the Balance

Many have discovered that advanced education, involving as it does the study of many subjects in depth, can lead to a serious challenge to Christian beliefs. Faced with the so-called 'rationalistic' approach of some otherwise skilful exponents of the various branches of science and, on the arts side, advanced studies in literature taking the student into German, French and Latin philosophy, shattering blows can rain down upon one's simple faith in God and His Word. I did not escape this experience and while I continued with the normal activities of the assembly, and outwardly all seemed well, there came a time when, as I prayed, the heavens seemed as brass and no answer came to the many questions I raised. The inner critical questioning rose and I found myself analysing and checking everything believed without difficulty in the past, until, for instance, I applied mathematical formulae to the measurements of Solomon's temple to see whether the Word of God was correct. To have admitted any of this to my parents I felt would have broken their hearts, but then the fear of being a hypocrite pressed harder and harder upon me until I felt I should lose my reason.

The crisis came one night when, unable to sleep for agony of mind, I got out of bed, threw myself on the floor and cried to God, 'If you are really God, then You can and will reveal Yourself to me.' From that moment all the questions died away and a great sense of calm came into my soul. My searching had finished and my faith returned, for God is all-powerful and yet had shown His care for me in my need. Looking back I am convinced that such coarse black strands in the pattern of life are permitted to serve as a contrasting back-cloth for the better display of the Golden Thread as it buries them in the weave and ends their domination.

University Guidance through War and Law

A day scholar's life at University during the 1914-1918 war was not easy. With many of the lecturers called to the colours, we had to travel around the four major colleges for lectures; take scanty midday meals 'on the move' as both time and meat were scarce (meat rations being required at home); work during the night until the early hours, often in air-raids when sleep would have been impossible in any case. But for me some of the inevitable departures from the common practices of years gave training and experience I was to need and be thankful for in later years.

Just as I began the four-year course, the law regulating teaching practice was altered to permit students undertaking a degree course to undergo their teaching practice in secondary schools. This was hailed as something of an advance in teacher training for the degree candidate, but already my heart was hearing the whisper of a call to missionary work and I was anxious to obtain the certificate for primary education in case the call grew clearer; I knew that to teach on the mission field I would need teaching experience and qualification in more general subjects. I sought an interview with the Professor to discover whether I could be sure of

Elsie Ransom, B.A. London

receiving the certificate for work in primary schools if I had done my teaching practice in a secondary school. Professor Adams could give no undertaking, much less a guarantee, that this would be the case because the law was so new and he thought that such changes often passed through difficult transition periods.

Much to the surprise of fellow students I decided to continue my practical work in the primary schools, with the result that at the conclusion of training I possessed not only the 'Dip Educ' but also the diploma for elementary teaching in addition to my degree. As far as I am aware mine was the only instance of this — but of far greater importance is it to record that the Golden Thread of God's guidance made a most vital series of stitches which as the years passed glistened more and more brightly. Not only did I need to know everything possible about primary teaching, with an accepted diploma for my school of Chinese girls, but the day came when I had to teach my own children when war prevented their attending any other school.

Prison Gold Thread

Times of war are times of shock, but one hardly expected to be informed at University that our kindly lecturer in Applied Mathematics, who was more than a lecturer, a devoted teacher with a constant care to help with our individual problems, had been sent to Wormwood Scrubs Prison! He had declined to have anything to do with war work and must pay the price in those days for his convictions. Knowing the man, our hearts were heavy, and I remember taking out my Bible in the bus on the way home and reading Psalm 18:30, 'As for God: His way is perfect,' and asking myself, 'Could the removal of Mr. G. B. Jeffries be one of those perfect ways?' Shortly afterwards I wrote him a letter expressing my sympathy for his suffering incurred for what he felt was pleasing to God. There was no

The author's parents, Mr. and Mrs. T. Ransom

The hospital at Wintertime. The Koll's home in Hinghwa, China

response until two years later, when the war was over, I received a letter from him saying that my message had not been received by him until he was released and now how glad he was to discover a Christian student in our somewhat atheistical college. By this time I had finished at college and only met him once at a meeting of the Mathematical Society just before leaving for China, when he wished me Godspeed in following the Master's call. I describe this discovery of a Christian friend via a prison sentence because thirty years later it was seen to be another sure stitch of the Golden Thread, as will be shown.

Chapter 4

Golden Thread Bugs

Upon leaving college I did 'supply teaching' on a temporary basis for two terms before taking my first permanent teaching job, a down-to-earth (and more) challenging task in a near-slum area of those days behind the Edgware Road. It was hard going indeed but provided just what I needed in many ways as I discovered how much nearer to the children one was able to get when contact with their teacher was the only bright spot in their drab lives. Nearness to some of the grimmer realities of human existence in the 'back streets' of large cities was brought home to me one day when I discovered bugs crawling on the neck of a sweet little girl who gleefully informed me that Granny had plenty more at home. What a gracious preparation for meeting the same creatures ensconced snugly in every cranny of houseboats and inns in China in later days.

But I was to learn more than the art of recognition, for the servant of the Lord needs to be ready to deal with evil for the relief of the needy around, and this elementary but distasteful lesson came my way at about the same time — in a Sunday School class in North Kensington. I can still recall the shivers I experienced when, after a small boy had given me his cap to mind, I saw the huge bug creeping inside it. Dare I touch it? It seemed to me an evil thing which must be overcome so, having nothing else handy as I stood there with my little room crowded with thirty small children, many without shoes and socks, I grasped the bug in my fingers and crushed it, continuing all the while to tell of the love of Jesus. How often I thought of that initiation as, many years later, I sat beside my own little ones in Chinese boats and with torch in one hand, picked the bugs off them with the other as they slept!

At this period I also felt directed to prepare in every way possible for life as a missionary should the Lord confirm the call I seemed already to have heard. St. John's Ambulance work, First Aid classes, Home-Nursing, Invalid Cookery are examples of the courses and activities with which I filled my evenings while Sunday School, Bible Class and such activities occupied my weekends.

Love on the Altar

Ask any real athlete and he or she will confirm that training calls for discipline, for sacrifice, which is why that great fore-runner of all Christian missionaires likens his preparation to service to that of the contender of his day for 'the prize,' as in Philippians 3:8-14 and other passages. A little training and discipline I have so far endeavoured to describe in the pattern of God's Golden Thread of guidance in my life; but I confess I find it very difficult to discuss a great crisis which came early in my teaching career. Its importance demands a place; as near as I came to self-sacrifice.

Before this incident my desire to serve the Lord in the foreign field was something which had grown with me, a something which had coloured all my decisions and choices while still remaining curiously intangible. Now a tangible object attracted my attentions but one diametrically opposed to my whispered and intangible call to service abroad.

I was taking an Easter holiday at a seaside resort where we had spent most of our childhood holidays and there met, after a lapse of eleven years, a young man who had been a childhood friend. He was a devoted Christian in our fellowship, a keen soul-winner, within two days of my own age, and a new and adult love for him was kindled in my heart. A voice within said, 'Now the Lord would not expect you to give up someone you really loved. You have only told your parents and two intimate friends about going to China. No one else would know if you decide to give it up. Surely to be a wife and a mother is the greatest calling for a Christian woman.' How I prayed for guidance! The text on my bedroom wall was 'Thou, Lord, only makest me dwell in safety' (Ps. 4:8).

During the holiday there was a conference in a neighbouring town and my friend asked my companion and me to go there with him. Then God spoke to me loud and clear as the very first speaker in the meeting read from Genesis, Chapter 22, 'Take thy son, thy only son . . . WHOM THOU LOVEST . . .' Whenever I see the first almond blossom against a clear blue sky, that moment returns to me, for as I gazed out of the window of that hall on that bright Spring day I knew that I must put even my love into the Master's hands.

We corresponded for a time and then at Whitsuntide he wrote pressing me to go to see him, which I did, although the journey was rendered difficult by a rail strike. When after supper we were left alone I knew that the moment had arrived for me to tell him that God had called me to China. I could not sleep at all that night and learned afterwards that neither could he. Yet we continued to correspond for a time, my prayer being that, if it were God's will, He might also call my friend to the China mission field; but this was not the way, so we decided to close this chapter of our lives.

A Command in the Night

Shortly after this experience the Golden Thread peeped out of the pattern again in a remarkable way. I heard a voice in the night saying quite clearly, 'Arise and be doing, and the Lord be with thee.' When I awoke doubts arose in my mind as to whether or not I had been dreaming but as I turned over the leaves of the daily text calendar — there it stood, 'Arise and be doing, and the Lord be with thee,' (I Chron. 22:16). Then I thought perhaps I had turned over the leaves of the calendar during the previous week and this text had remained in my mind, even unconsciously. So I besought the Lord to be very gracious and show me in some way in which I could not be the agent, if it really was His voice to me.

It was the Lord's day so, as usual, we gathered around the Lord at His Table in the morning and came together again in the afternoon to teach the little ones. After Sunday School my former teacher put something into my hand saying, 'The Lord told me to give you this.' I opened the slip of paper and read, 'Arise and be doing, and the Lord be with thee!' I thanked God and took courage; and immediately enrolled with an evening course at the School of Oriental Studies of the University to learn Chinese. I did this in the full knowledge that such action would inevitably lead to a crucial test for that perennial physical problem of mine — eyesight.

Chinese Eye-Strain

There can be little doubt that Chinese is one of the most difficult languages to acquire because, as the reader will know, there is no alphabet from which to build words. Each word, a 'character' is made up of one or more strokes which must fit into a perfect square, and each of these has therefore to be individually memorised. Discerning such detail is taxing to normally healthy eyes so in my case provided an ideal physical 'test-bench' as to my fitness for China, for to serve there I must have the language. I therefore decided to study hard to put my eyes to maximum strain.

As I was each day doing full-time teaching and travelling at least twice a week to college in the evening immediately after school, there was little time for real study, so I made a practice of carrying in my handbag a pack of small square cards each inscribed with a Chinese character to be memorised. By shuffling the cards and turning them one by one, I could learn them as I travelled in train or bus. After two years spent in this way, I applied to my eye specialist for a prescription for the eye drops which I had always to use for several days prior to an examination. At the appointment, I told her I wanted, on this occasion, a very clear and careful opinion as to the state of my eyes but would not tell her my reason for the request. She smiled at me and said, 'You want to go to the mission field?' Quite taken aback, I said, 'But how can you know this, for no one has been told except my parents and a few close friends?' She then revealed that my father had told her the story related in the first chapter in this book — and she had remembered. I feared this might lead her to give a biased opinion but she promised to tell me the absolute truth. After the examination she said, 'Your eyes are better than I have ever found them on any previous occasion.' Thus I believed the Lord confirmed that I was on the road of His will.

Chapter 5

Shock Release for China

The 'all clear' for my eyes after straining at Chinese characters was for me a divine 'permission to proceed' but it was followed by an almost disconcerting acceleration of my programme. (Although the events of this chapter reveal a remarkable series of opening doors, one still hesitates to claim that all was the pure gold of the thread of God's guidance, since here and there it seems likely there were strands of less glorious colour interwoven. One must not speak glibly of the Golden Thread.)

The end of my second year of Chinese study almost coincided with the completion of my fourth year's work as a teacher. One evening in June, my father came home from a meeting and surprised me by saying he had arranged for me to go to tea the next day at the home of a missionary from one of our stations in China in order to meet a young nurse who was preparing to leave for our mission hospital in Hinghwa in the autumn. This appointment was unwelcome to me for I was working intensively for two important examinations in Chinese shortly due and needed all spare time for study, but anxious not to hurt Father, I kept it. There I met the nurse who was later to become a close friend. We met again at the Saturday evening Bible Class where the message was from Mark, Chapter 1. After the class she came to me and said, 'Verse 18 is for you: leave your nets and come out to China with me in the autumn!'

This came as a shock to me for I had still to complete an agreed fifth year of professional teaching in return for a free University education. In those days this undertaking was given under oath. The idea of going out to China in the company of a friend greatly appealed to me, so after much thinking and prayer, I wrote to the Minister of Education explaining something of the circumstances and asking if I might be released from the fifth year of my contract. We had heard that there was precedent for a release in cases where teaching would be continued overseas but these seemed confined to British Empire countries, not economically remote countries like China.

My application was made just before the summer vacation in late July but there was no reply of any kind from Whitehall by the end of the four weeks break. The new term began and I told my headmistress of my letter and an expected reply. There was still no news by the second week in September so, being worried about her responsibility to apply for a replacement should I leave, she sent me to visit Whitehall in person to enquire what was happening. I had no appointment but was eventually permitted to see an official who, after hearing my case including the facts that the boat for China was scheduled to leave on October 12th and that there was only one berth available, making the need for decision urgent, informed me that there would be no meeting of the appropriate Committee until later in October. He tried, however, to assure me that I could leave without further difficulty since at that particular time there was a glut of teachers 'on the market.' I explained that I could not accept such a situation because, if God wished me to go to China, He would make the way clear and I was not prepared to go out by a back door. This appeared to be the end of the discussion and I prepared to take leave when he called me back saying he would discuss the problem with another official, if I would wait.

Presently the same gentleman returned to give me 'his word of honour' that it was quite safe for me to leave my post. I felt uneasy so insisted that unless I had release from the fifth year of the contract in writing I would not book my passage to China on this boat. I felt the need to protect my parents against the future contingency of being required to refund the cost of my training. I left with little hope of a solution; the door seemed to be tightly shut. I was in for a surprise, however, for when I reached home for lunch the next day Father produced a sealed document delivered by courier from Whitehall — my release from the fifth year of teaching service!

Perfect Timing and Bible Class Faith

By now it was September 11th, leaving me just time to give my month's notice and be aboard the vessel for China on October 12th in the company of my nurse friend and the other missionary, who was returning to the work at the same time. The four weeks were full of buying the necessary outfit, packing, finishing my daily school work and bidding farewell to many friends. Among the latter, the Saturday Bible Class stands out in memory for was it not here that Christian fellowship had been such a stabilising factor in early days? And now these valued friends had saved the 50 pounds to pay my fare to China, an appreciable sum in 1923, and even more so, bearing in mind that most of them were hard-working laundry or factory operatives from poor homes in North Kensington (where our assembly flourished), ardent Christians having little or nothing of fellowship at home. Certainly this love and share in the mission work is inscribed permanently in those records which the Lord will open in a future day.

'East of Suez' New Life of all Kinds

The journey out was full of wonder for one who had never left the shores of England before: the storm-riven passage across the Bay of Biscay contrasted by the blue calm of the Mediterranean with its first view of Gibralter; the homely day ashore in Marseilles, meeting two of our former China missionaries, the sullen majesty of the smoking Stromboli volcano, the progress through the colourful Strait of Messina; all leading up to our first touch with the East at Port Said.

Then followed the slow trip through the Suez Canal with its leisurely panorama of desert shore life complete with camels padding along in seeming endless procession, the parched dried look of Aden, so uninviting that we did not go ashore; all giving place to the grand swell of the Indian Ocean which brought us to Bombay and our first smell of the Far East with the heat, the flies and the characteristic conglomeration of traffic comprising all conceivable types of transport from ox-carts to motor cars mixed in endless confusion. Down the coast of India now we came to Ceylon (now Sri Lanka), seeing there more luxurious vegetation which brings its own peculiar enchantment to equatorial regions, and there, in Colombo we permitted ourselves the experience of a visit to the temple of the great reclining Buddha (having to remove our shoes at the door!). We were on our way again to Singapore where we had our introduction to more Chinese than so far seen, as they were well represented among the Malay population: in retrospect all a graciously gradual but sure insertion of new labourers into their sphere of service for the Lord.

New Currents — New Winds

As we turned the corner of South Asia to go up from

Singapore to Hong Kong, I felt a little queasy for the first time since leaving home; a physical effect of the strong currents which mark the approach to the East China Sea which would be our northward course until we reached the end of our long sea voyage and stepped ashore at Shanghai at the end of November after six weeks afloat. In order to give us a taste of, and some acclimatisation to life in China before reaching our mission station at Hinghwa, Mr. H. Ruck, the missionary who met us at Shanghai had arranged that we should travel to Chinkiang on a Japanese steamer, Chinese fare, instead of using the railway.

Adaptation to the new Chinese bedding roll laid on the hard wooden bunks would not unduly worry the new missionary for had she not 'Youth on her side?' But as we lay and watched the cockroaches climbing up the walls, corresponding shivers passed down our spines: yet 'twas all part of the calculated insertions of new labourers' into the environment of their work. As the years passed, we grew accustomed to this, and worse, as an unnoticed back-cloth to experience. On this journey, also, we had our first initiation into Chinese food eaten with chop-sticks. I say 'we' but in truth my friend was not able to leave her bunk for long.

At Chinkiang, which is the Yangtse River port at the junction with the Grand Canal, we transferred to a Chinese sailing boat and so became acquainted with the mode of transport which would in future be ours whenever we had to leave our missionary station since it is an island. The cramped little cabins of these vessels are fitted with two wooden benches which serve as beds at night. As we made this first journey in the winter, we did not have much trouble with the ever present bugs but we were to learn later that travelling in the summer was entirely different in this respect. Then we learned the meaning of two Chinese words 'ting feng' and 'suen feng' — 'contrary wind' and 'favourable wind.' In 'ting feng' conditions, the boat was pulled along by boatmen with tow ropes fastened around their bodies, trudging along the towpath ashore at a pace calculated to facilitate the picking of daisies on the banks had there been daisies to pick and had the means of disembarkation not been far too perilous for us landlubbers to attempt! 'Ting feng' so predominated that it took us more than a week to reach the smelly little harbour of the City of Hinghwa, our destination and our new 'home.' The nearby East Gate was my quarter for residence while the nurse was taken on to the North Gate Hospital inside the city wall.

Thus were we prepared physically for the changing currents and contrary winds of our new country and I believe granted object lessons in the need for bracing up to similar elements in the far more important spiritual circumstances of our service. Perhaps we were learning that stitches of the Golden Thread could be as surely woven in unstable seas and the intangibly turbulent air as in the more solid substance of our lives on 'mother earth.'

Chapter 6

Teaching and Learning Lessons at Hinghwa

M any are the fears which press upon the heart as one begins daily living in a heathen country: one misses the moral atmosphere which pervades even a nominally Christian country and provides an element in which to adjust to problems. The first of these in China is adjustment to the strange language and I was not long in discovering that my Peking classical Mandarin had to be considerably modified to fit into the new dialect. The only teacher available to me was a fine old Confucian scholar who had no idea how to do anything other than study the volumes of the Sacred Edict, so after the winter months when I realised that very little progress had been made under his instruction, I consulted with my fellow-workers and agreed that I should start school. Learning to speak a new language is very like learning to swim — after memorising the 'strokes,' take the plunge.

A senior missionary, Mrs. Ruck, who had been born in China and therefore spoke perfect Chinese, volunteered to help me and thus, in April, 1924, 'The Wisdom and Virtue School for Girls' opened with seven pupils, four older girls and three little ones. We chose two adjacent rooms connected by a sliding window, through which medicine had been sold when the building had served as a temporary hospital, so that through the hatch I could ask what expression to use when a difficulty arose. Slowly the words began to come and by June, when my helper had to leave to take her children up to the mountains, I could manage alone. This I did until we closed for the hot summer period some weeks later.

A Secret Threat Removed

As the ladies of the household and their children had left for the hills, Mr. Ruck went to sleeping quarters in the hospital building and my nurse friend came across to the East Gate house where I lived as it was not permissible for a gentleman to sleep in the same house as unmarried ladies. This change resulted in much of my time being occupied with our friendship and already, in the first six months of my service, I had begun to realise that this was no help to me. Rather was there a danger of it sapping my spiritual life and the new arrangement led to a conviction in my soul that I must seek deliverance. But how? I well recollect the hot, humid morning on which I knelt down in distress and prayed that the Lord would set me free; that I was willing for anything if only I could be enabled to put Him and His work first, and that I felt the possessiveness of my friend was hindering this. Little did I know how near was the answer to my prayer!

The nurse was on duty during the daytime at the hospital but it was noticed that during the evenings she had a very severe cough and was running a high temperature. During the afternoon of the same day of my early morning prayer the mission doctor insisted upon examining her and discovered that she had contracted tuberculosis and had it very badly: the hot, humid climate had been too much for her. It happened that the doctor was about to join his wife for a short

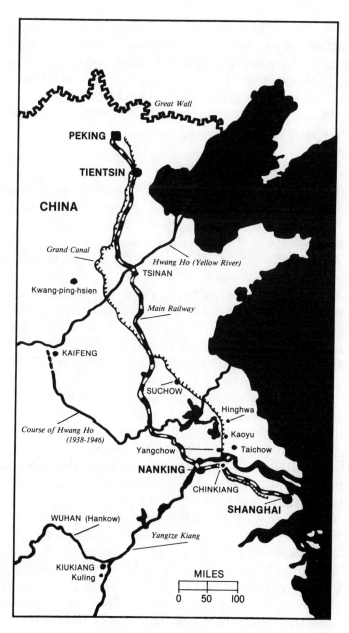

Map showing extent of the mission work in northeast China

respite in the mountains so it was resolved to take my friend up to a sanatorium, provided I would go with her since the Chinese moral code would not permit her to travel alone with the doctor. Thus, within twenty-four hours of that morning prayer we were on our way out of the mission station to which the nursing sister was never able to return.

Secret Questions — and Answers

The upheaval all this caused in my mission work in the following three years is difficult, even now, to measure. It led me to take stock, not so much of the practical aspects of the work but of my own position spiritually relative to the will of the Lord. Had I made a mistake in coming out to China so hurriedly? Had I acted from a mixed motive in wishing to have the company of a friend rather than face a lonely road? In this connection, a verse of Scripture I had never before noticed came to my attention, 'He gave them their request (the desires of their heart); but sent leanness into their soul' (Psalm 106:15). Then again I questioned, 'Ought I never to have sought release from my oath to complete five years teaching service in England?' Again came along a verse hitherto unnoticed by me in Psalm 15 where, in answer to the beautifully rhetorical question of verse 1, 'Lord, who shall abide in thy tabernacle? Who shall dwell in thy holy hill?' David replies 'He that sweareth to his own hurt, and changeth not' (verse 4).

Why? is a question often difficult to answer, but it arose again and again in my heart; 'Why had God so miraculously set me free if I ought not to have come to China?' The scriptures quoted above had become mine after long searching and seemed to confirm the validity of my self-interrogation. Perhaps the Lord saw that I needed this discipline — hence the upheavals with their resulting personal investigation. There, for the time being, I had to leave any effort to find the Golden

Thread amid the rather tangled skein of my life at that juncture.

'Gideonic' Test and Gracious Confirmation

After the summer weeks in the mountains, spent for the most part at the bedside of my friend, I returned to Hinghwa free to begin the new school term. I was encouraged to find the numbers so increased that I needed to engage a young Chinese Christian helper. She had a very interesting background as the youngest daughter of Mr. Li, an old opium smoker whose whole life had been transformed when he found the Lord Jesus Christ as the One who could not only forgive his sins but who had the power to deliver him from their power over him, especially that of opium smoking. Mr. Li's recovery was such that he was able to resume his trade as a watch repairer and so lift his family from the depths of poverty into which his addiction had reduced them. This daughter had in consequence been able to receive some education and, in fact, proved to be my right-hand helper throughout the years of service in the Chinese school.

The school now so increased in numbers that we had to convert every available room in the building into class rooms. This seemed good but after a little time there appeared to be so little real fruit on the spiritual plane that one began again to wonder whether it was really God's will to continue.

This questioning shortly came to a head when it became clear also that there was insufficient money in the bank to pay the next month's wages. I then took Mrs. Ruck into my confidence but asked her not to discuss the matter with her husband as I wished to see the Lord's hand in it all, unmoved by human planning. So we prayed together, asking that if the Lord wanted the schoolwork to continue He would send along the money needed for the next month's payments. A day or two later Mrs. Ruck told me that her husband had asked her if the school was in need of funds, assuring me that she had not mentioned our need to him. A gift was then made to us for the school from the general missionary funds for the first time.

My heart was not quite satisfied that no hint of our need had been given, though perhaps unconsciously, so I continued to pray that the Lord would confirm the matter through another channel. Shortly after this a gift of about the same amount came to hand from my old Sunday School in North Kensington, England! Even so I argued within myself that the thoughtful friends 'back home' had possibly felt that as a matter of routine giving it was time to remember me. So, like Gideon with his fleece (Judges 6:36-40), I besought the Lord to be very gracious to me and send me an answer from some place which could not know about our particular need. Sure enough, before the end of the month there came a gift of about the same amount from Kamloops, British Columbia, Canada — a gift from someone of whom I had no knowledge and had never even heard before!

Thus many questions and healthy though anxious exercises were answered and the Golden Thread seemed again readily discernable in the midst of the weave, so strongly as to keep the school open and thriving for many a year. Better still, many dear girls found the Lord Jesus as their Saviour in 'The Wisdom and Virtue School for Girls' in Hinghwa.

Chapter 7

Civil Commotion and the King's Enemies

Throughout the three years, 1924 to 1927, the Lord's blessing, witnessed by a steady growth of the school and expansion of the staff, was punctuated by a sequence of difficult journeys during holiday periods, mostly visiting the sick friend in the sanatorium up in the mountains. Even in normal times this journey involved a week of travel but the period was politically stormy in China. Could it be that, as is not unusual in His ways, the Lord's direction of His Golden Thread drew me in and out through a web of dangerous but edifying experiences in 'vacation' to keep His servant spiritually tensile in a period of blessing? One sometimes sees it so.

After the autumn term in 1924, the friends on the mission station felt that I should pay a visit to the sick one in the mountains during the January-February holiday of 1925, the Chinese New Year break, since the only other lengthy school holiday in China occurs in the hot summer period of July-August. Consequently in January I set out from our island of Hinghwa, starting with two days on a little houseboat on which one's only bed is a wadded quilt on the hard boards serving as seats during the day.

At Chinkiang, where we joined the mighty Yangtse River which is too wide here to permit a view of the opposite shore, I sought out the house on the hill where another of our missionaries, Mademoiselle Junod, lived. Before taking further transport, I settled for a good night on a soft bed but at 5 a.m. we were rudely awakened by loud reports. In answer to my call to the next room, Mlle. Junod said the noise was only that of fireworks connected with some festival but as we later sat at breakfast I glanced out of the window in time to see a cannon wheeled up to our front gate and open fire on some distant target. As I commented, 'Look at your fireworks . . .' the return fire began to strike into our house. Unsuspected by us we were in the midst of a civil war, so Mlle. Junod said, 'I will go up the hill to see what the American missionaries are doing about the situation.' I insisted upon accompanying her and, as we neared the house, a bullet passed over Mlle. Junod's shoulder and splintered the plaster on the gate post. Then to our dismay we discovered that the U. S. Consul had withdrawn all their nationals down to the town during the night and we were left stranded. Upon return to our house, the little Chinese amah announced that bullets had gone through the larder window and pierced a cocoa tin.

What to do? First Mlle. Junod searched for a Swiss flag to fly from the roof and, although nothing more official than a gala flag depicting William Tell shooting the apple on his son's head, this was mounted on the chimney though later it was the subject of much confusion among many folk who could not conceive what country it represented! Next we packed our bedding rolls with emergency garments and, having done what we could, got onto our knees to ask the Lord for the next step. While we were praying there came a knock on the door and, to our joy, a young missionary from the China Inland Mission in the town said they had realised our position and he had volunteered to fetch us. With a Chinese carrying pole on his shoulders, he carried our bundles as we walked down the hill to the Foreign Concession which had been enclosed with electrified barbed wire usual at such times. We were lodged at the offices of the Asiatic Petroleum Company and the following day the 'war' was over, witnessed by the flags of the latest triumphant war-lord flying on the houses and shops of the city.

The following night, therefore, saw Mlle. Junod and me conducted out through the barbed wire and on to the quay to await the arrival of the Japanese up-river steamer. Two days of this brought us to the big river port of Kiukiang from which we could reach the foothills of the mountains where my friend lay in the hospital. Up we went, this final phase of our journey, carried in sedan chairs through deep snow, amid icicles hanging from the rocks and over narrow slippery paths across over-hanging precipices; up the thousand steps until we reached Kuling, the resort 5,000 feet above the plain and so to the sanatorium.

Through Waves, Clouds and Storms

'God gently clears the way; we wait His time . . .' so goes the 300-year-old hymn by Gerhardt and so it was in 1925 and is today as we seek the Golden Thread of His guidance. The first half of the year passed seemingly very quickly as the school increased in numbers and the Sunday School was built up. At the end of June it was decided that as soon as school closed for the summer vacation I should again make the trip to the mountains to visit our sick nurse.

When living 'up country' as at Hinghwa, we seldom had clear news of what was taking place along the coast or in the big coastal ports so on this occasion we were quite unprepared for man-made hazards, aided and abetted, as it turned out, by vagaries of weather. All went well as we made the two-day journey in the small boat to the big river. I was accompanied by a local woman who had helped as a school cleaner — for 'ladies do not travel alone in China.' There, however, a great storm arose and although our boatman attempted to cross the river because sunset was almost upon us, the waves beat us back to an anchorage near some of the big sea-going salt junks. The captain of one of these offered to take us across and so, taking our own Hinghwa boatman with us, we changed over into the large cabin of the junk.

For the first time I really experienced sea-sickness as we tossed in that storm but this paled into insignificance as I gathered by listening to the talk of the crew that there was trouble ashore, trouble for 'foreigners.' There had been an anti-foreign revolt. Foreigners had been turned out of their homes, their furniture piled in the streets and burned, the British Consul had been man-handled, and as we drew near the port we could hear the shouts of 'Kill the foreign devils!' Our boatman told me to keep out of sight because of my yellow hair. The captain and he decided to anchor out in mid-stream for the night: a night never to be forgotten as I lay on the hard wooden plank, no bedding this time and my handbag for a pillow, alone with my sickness and my thoughts. With my little woman companion sleeping across my feet so that I should have warning of any attempt to assault or throw me overboard, and no light in the dark cabin except the glowing ends of the crew's cigarettes, I contemplated the ugly fact that as no one in the port knew of my arrival, my friends up country would have no news of anything happening to me until long after the event.

Golden Light on a Grey Dawn

As dawn grew grey I managed to find a chink between the boat boards where I could glimpse my 'Daily Light' book from my handbag and read, 'I will both lay me down in peace, and sleep; for thou, Lord, only makest me dwell in safety' (Psalm 4:8). When it grew lighter, the crew of the junk told me that unless I could contact my people in the port and get off the boat, they would take me far away up river and backed up this statement by demanding a large sum of money quite beyond anything I had with me. I therefore scribbled a note on an odd piece of paper, addressed it to Mlle. Junod at the China Inland Mission and, waking my somewhat reluctant boatman, told him to go ashore and deliver it. He protested because it was raining but, deciding that my only umbrella was less important than my life I gave this to him as he departed with much grumbling.

Minutes dragged by like hours and it was already 8 a.m. before there came a knock on the boards of the boat and a voice calling 'Miss Ransom!' At first I hardly dared peep out lest it should be a trick to sieze me but as the knocking continued I opened a small crack in the boarding and there stood the British Consul with an armed guard. Obviously very nervous, he bade me hurry away. I explained about the money demanded and at once he advanced this and we hastened ashore, through the barbed wire barrier, past the charred furniture lying in the streets and into a large foreign house in which all the foreign women and children were gathered while the men patrolled the Concession with rifles. All exclaimed when they saw my pallor, made me lie down on a couch and plied me with hot soup, the first food for many hours. Hardly had I time to take a spoonful than orders arrived for all women and children to board a steamer specially chartered for Shanghai — exactly in the opposite direction I had wished to go! By this time Mlle. Junod had joined the party so, sleeping in the smoking room of the vessel all night we arrived in Shanghai, there to await some opportunity of going up river again.

It was about ten days later that I reached the mountains and after this tortuous journey saw my sick friend again. Alas, she was not getting better and most of my summer time was spent at her bedside. The doctor would not allow us to tell her that there was little hope of her being able to return to the mission station. It was indeed a difficult situation for she was always expressing the hope of returning to her work. As for me it was, to say no more, another very practical lesson in patience and how to 'Bear ye one another's burdens' (Galatians 6:2).

Chapter 8

Through Lupus to Love in the Lord

Autumn again brought a joyous return to day school and Sunday School, both still blessedly growing. We now had seventy day school pupils and a proportionate expansion on Sundays. In common with the day school in the city, our school was closed on Wednesday afternoons — and we also had school on Saturdays. This Wednesday afternoon freedom from teaching was used by the Lord to expand the mission work to a village two miles distant from Hinghwa through a meshing of circumstances which surely only the Lord's Golden Thread can achieve. Was it not He who said, 'I will make you to become fishers of men?' (Mark 1:17)

At this village lived a farmer's wife, Mrs. Han, who during the summer season left her wattle and mud house every day to sell radishes and other vegetables grown on the farm, in the city of Hinghwa. On this journey one day she saw some clothing floating on a patch of water but upon closer examination discovered a young woman attempting to commit suicide by drowning. Mrs. Han rescued the poor girl with a punt pole, took her home and cared for her and when she was fit persuaded her to return to her home. Alas, this girl was but another case of circumstances we often encountered in China — when daughter-in-law could no longer bear life with mother-in-law and would try to take her own life to revenge herself because the husband's family would by law be compelled to pay compensation to her own family! In this case, however, the rescued girl had lived under Christian influence in Chinkiang and knew a little of the work of the missionaries and, wondering what she might do by way of thanking Mrs. Han, had persuaded her to visit our hospital for treatment of the infectious facial disease, Lupus, from which the old lady suffered. The Lord had used the loving care shown her in the skill of the doctor and in the daily dressings undertaken by Mr. Koll to enable her to find the One who loved her more, until she opened her heart to the Saviour.

This all had happened before I arrived in China and, as seems so often the case in His ordering, the way for further blessing had been opened in advance. When Mrs. Han discovered that we had Wednesday afternoons free, she offered us the use of her courtyard for children's meetings. So Mrs. Ruck and I went off in a boat to make a start. But the enemy was not going to permit so easy an invasion of his domain and tried his old weapon in heathen lands, superstitious fear, to hinder our work.

We carried the plain wooden benches of the house out into the open air of the yard, dusted them, rang a bell and waited for the children to come in, for they had all said they would like to come. But no one dared to come. Little heads peeped round the straw fences but no one ventured to come in and sit down. When we asked the reason, we were told that when the children saw us dusting the seats, they thought we were smearing them with something which would make their souls stick so that they wouldn't be able to get out again! The following Wednesday we set off again with the blackboard and harmonium but this time with a sample of our best singers from the day school. The routine was repeated but after dusting the seats we put our own children through exercises, rising and sitting to command, to demonstrate the non-stick quality of the seat surfaces. Gradually the little crowd gathered into the seats in the yard and from then, week after week, we were able to hold the meeting telling all the time of the love of God through Jesus Christ our Lord. Surely 'that Day' will reveal the eternal blessings accruing from Mrs. Han's opened heart which opened her yard.

Straining to a Break

During that term a new nurse arrived from Germany to work in the hospital. She was a sister of our surgeon and came to take the place of the sick girl, a considerable relief to our medical missionary services. While this was a matter for thankfulness in our whole missionary work, it had the 'side effect' of increasing a burden private to myself. For some time I had felt the increasing difficulty of writing daily letters to the sanatorium hinting at the sad fact that the patient would never be able to return to Hinghwa, but now that a replacement nurse had actually taken duty this burden became more than a merely difficult and irksome task, it developed into enervating strain. This together with additional work in the course of our expanding service and other problems of the time combined to lead me, almost unwittingly, into a 'nervous breakdown' marked by inability to sleep and a complete loss of voice.

Mercifully, Mrs. Ruck and the Chinese teachers were able to carry on the school work while kind friends helped me on to the road of recovery. At this point I insisted that the doctor of the sanatorium should make it clear to my sick friend that she could not return to our station which was very hot and damp in summer time as it lay well below sea level. Meanwhile our own doctor in Hinghwa also insisted that I must have a break from visiting her in the hospital with the result that, when school finished, the new nurse and I were sent off to holiday in a seaside place in North China where we were offered the use of a little bungalow for the summer. The Lord knew it was just what I needed and, after a truly wonderful rest and relaxing sea-bathing, the whole holiday was capped by a few days in Peking and I returned full of renewed strength to face a new term at school.

Sanatorium S.O.S.

Hardly had I reached Hinghwa after the long journey from the north before a telegram arrived begging me to go to the mountains as my nurse friend had become very ill indeed. Not having unpacked after my latest trip I was able to set off almost immediately on yet another memorable journey, this time accompanied by Mr. Ruck, who was going up to bring his wife and children home. First came the familiar sail down to the big river junction in a very small houseboat. Then followed a nightmare ride in a rickety car on a very bad road in order to reach the ferry in time for the last night crossing to Chinkiang, a long wait on the pier for the upriver steamer and finally a moonlight climb up the mountain by the four bearers who carried me in the sedan chair.

Red Emergency

At that time our mission surgeon, Dr. Neuffer, was also on the mountain with his family, when news came through that the Red Army was approaching the mountain heights from the south side. Quick decision was called for as he must avoid being confined to the mountain tops and cut off from his hospital work, perhaps for months. What then were we to do with the sick nurse who stood at risk of being segregated from us all. Her case seemed hopeless so Dr. Neuffer asked me to approach the sanatorium doctor to ask whether a trip down the mountain to live on the plain would hasten her end or not. The verdict was that at this stage nothing could make much difference to her condition, so a long litter was hastily constructed from bamboo and the next day we set out.

The doctor walked alongside the patient's litter, having administered an injection of morphia as we started, and my chair followed immediately behind. Arriving safely down on the plain, we had to wait to enquire whether the captain of the down-river steamer would be willing to take such a case aboard his boat. We were thankful when he agreed although this was on condition that the patient was kept on deck and that we did not take her into any cabin. After two days journey down the Yangtse River, we were met by an ambulance from the hospital in the river port of Chinkiang, in response to a telegram from our doctor. We were able to leave our sick friend at the hospital under good care while we all made the last few days trip up the Grand Canal to our own mission station.

It is not always easy to see the Golden Thread being securely woven into the sometimes dark fabric of life . . . but experience in God's Faculty of Christianity was beginning to teach me that it is invariably there.

Chapter 9

Ordered Out
of China
by God and Man

The last term at school was a good one, ending with a very happy Prize Day in January, 1927. Yet as we closed I had the very strong feeling that something of importance to me was about to happen; there was for me an indefinable atmosphere of impending change in the air. I well remember, in sharp outline, an incident not in itself unusual in the China of that day but which, as I look back, teaches joyful preservation in the midst of inclement conditions. The doctor's sister and I decided to pay a visit to Mr. and Mrs. Gustav Koll at one of our out-stations although the weather was so bitterly cold that our boatman had to break the ice in front of our boat to cut a passage as we went along.

At the close of two days of hard rowing, we noticed that the boatman's wife who was standing up, plying the long oar in a sculling motion at the stern of the boat, seemed exceptionally anxious to reach our destination that night instead of adopting the more leisurely course of mooring overnight at the shore-side of some small village. We disembarked safely having accomplished the journey without another night afloat but in the morning we were amazed to learn that the dear woman had given birth to a son during the night! Of course I went down to the boat to pay a visit and there she was, lying on the hard bed-board, her face beaming satisfaction. Not a thought was given to heating in the freezing cold but when I asked where the baby was she plunged her hand into her wadded gown and drew him out all wrapped in red swaddling bands.

Upon our return to Hinghwa, we were greeted with the news that our sick nurse friend must be removed from the hospital in Chinkiang and taken to the coast because the Red Army was approaching. A council of our workers was held and it was decided that in all the circumstances of the case, the sick sister should be taken back to Holland. As we pondered the problem, there seemed no one available for this task other than myself; so although it was a great sorrow for me to think of leaving my school work just as it was building up so nicely, I volunteered to go and with a somewhat heavy heart began to pack my belongings. Did the Golden Thread appear a little tarnished? That the decision was a right one was confirmed the next morning by a notice from the British Consul in Shanghai ordering all British subjects to leave the interior of China. Another elderly missionary and I were the only British on our station!

By the morning I had packed all my possessions; received the good wishes of my colleagues at a hastily arranged farewell gathering at the hospital to bid me Godspeed as I left, sick at heart, the home and work where I had been so happy, expecting to see it no more. Little could I guess that God would prepare that very place as a home for me and my family for many a year to come!

Friends Indeed at Shanghai!

Again it was Mr. Ruck, who accompanied me to Shanghai, where we arrived at the station to find soldiers with large battle-axes standing on guard. With all my luggage on a wheelbarrow, we trudged off to find the home of Mr. Willis senior. There Mr. Ruck asked if they would take me as a refugee because the missionary homes were surely already full. Then the seed of a lifelong friendship was sown in a moment as a gentle voice called from one of the bedrooms. 'There is room in my bed,' and in I went to meet Helen Willis for the first time; still known and loved as I write this nearly fifty years on.

How kind they all were to me as I waited there for the four months it took to find a boat which would accept the sick girl on board — four months of war during which new refugees arrived daily at the Willis home. Every day I visited the sick sister in the local hospital although the road there led along the border of the Foreign Concession which was subject to sniper fire from the roofs of adjoining houses. But it was a time of learning for me, learning the love of these new friends who called me their Shanghai daughter, a love which gave an insight into a selfless care for all who need shelter. Some of these arrived with children, some with birds in cages, others with clocks and mattresses (stuffed under our bed), and some with all their food stores thrown into a sheet tied up by the four corners. At last came a whole family with several children including a month-old baby, which signalled the moment for Helen and me to give up the bedroom and retire to sleep on the dining room chairs.

In May, the sick girl was pronounced 'germ free' and we obtained a passage on a cargo vessel carrying only sixteen passengers and with all cabins on deck level which ensured us plenty of fresh air. With a large lump in my throat, I glimpsed the last of China's shores knowing that my work for the time was ended there after only three and a half years. What was God planning for me?

Adrift Ashore at Singapore

But my duties on board left little time for sad reflection. By the time we passed the Philippines, the sick nurse became very ill again and it was no easy task to nurse and keep her segregated from other passengers. She had been ill for three years, her heart rebelled against having to leave China and it was hard for her to cooperate with someone much younger than herself. The emotional strain of all this combined with the tropical heat aggravated the disease until her condition caused much anxiety and at 6 o'clock on the morning of our arrival in Singapore, I was summoned to the Captain's cabin and told by the ship's doctor that we must leave the ship. There was no time to lose as after a hasty packing of the absolute necessities, a breaking of the news to the patient, a sigh of prayer to the only One who could help, we were lowered into a small boat for the shore. At my insistence, the ship's doctor went with us to the State Hospital where a new problem faced me as they asked for the name of our Mission Society. My statement that we had none brought a refusal to take the responsibility of admitting the sick one as a patient, for how could they be sure that the bill would be paid? As we had planned to go right through to Rotterdam on the same vessel, I had very little ready money with me but I placed what I had (a five-pound note) on the counter and the official accepted it for a few days' guarantee.

At my request, the hospital doctor put me into a rickshaw and directed it to the Y.W.C.A. as it was late afternoon and I could not speak Malay, nor did I know anything of Singapore other than that it was no place for a young woman to be wandering around alone at night. However, I soon became aware that the rickshaw coolie had made up his mind to make the most of me by wandering all through the native quarters of the city on the pretense of finding the Y.W.C.A. I began to feel afraid but at last saw in the distance another rickshaw whose occupant had a nice crop of curly hair. Knowing by this that he was neither Chinese or Malay, I called out in English for help and found indeed he was a young Englishman who said the Y.W.C.A. was, in fact, only just round the corner and that the rickshaw coolie surely knew this in spite of his protestations of ignorance. The young man came with us and I was soon safely inside the home. I begged the hostess to pay off the coolie with the correct fare who, cheated of his excessive charges for a long unnecessary run, departed in a fury. Although the hostess told me she could not officially give me accommodation as the hostel was for business girls, upon hearing my predicament, she found me temporary sleeping room in place of a resident then on holiday. The thermometer was reading over 80°F in the little shower room and the water from the cold tap seemed nigh boiling — but the Lord had protected me and provided a sleeping place in a city in which I was truly a stranger.

At breakfast the next morning, I made a point of discovering the Malay word for the cheapest fare on a tramcar for I dare not risk another rickshaw episode. Off I went to find my way to the shipping offices, the shopping area and the hospital, by travelling in the 'native' section of the tramcar, taking a ticket for 'annam' and then booking another 'annam,' and so on, until I arrived where I wished to be. My first task was to send a cable to Mr. Voorhoeve at the Hague, Holland, asking for funds. I was quite inexperienced in this kind of work and had no money to waste on expensive telegrams, but here again the Lord stood by me. As I planned the wording and form-filling, a gentleman touched me on the shoulder and asked if I needed help: a complete stranger, yet the Lord's messenger. He worded the message clearly and briefly, told me how to dispatch it by 'delayed wire,' disappeared and I never saw him again. A day or two later, the money I needed was dispatched in the Bank of the Netherlands and from that time, for nearly a month, I toured the shipping offices seeking some shipping company to take the nurse home.

In the meantime at the hospital, our patient was receiving regular injections which were resulting in some improvements in her condition and at last I obtained promise of a passage to Marseilles, France, on a P & O Line boat on condition that the ship's doctor on arrival in Singapore would give his consent which, of course, we would not be sure of until the last moment.

Mercies Abound to Marseilles

Mercifully we were accepted on the appointed vessel and, with the much needed help of some kind Christian friends I had discovered in an assembly (by walking around the streets of Singapore one Sunday morning until I heard familiar hymns being sung), I got my sick friend aboard in time for sailing.

In the light of past experience I kept her in our cabin until we had passed Colombo in Ceylon, now Sri Lanka, as I knew that after that point we could not be turned off the ship until we reached Port Said. On this matter our prayers were answered and we were able to retain our berth to the end of the voyage at Marseilles. This diversion off our course through France (for we had set off from Shanghai, it will be remembered, booked right through to Holland) again cast us upon the Lord's direct help, for my French had receded into the background during the years in which I had been speaking Chinese and German on the mission station and I felt clueless as to what would happen as we disembarked in France to make our way over land to Holland. However, I found I had with me the home address of Mlle. Junod, who was then returning to Europe via America, so from Port Said I telegraphed this address for advice.

We reached Marseilles and I well recollect my feelings

as I waited on deck for the ship to dock, with a prayer in my heart and scanning the groups of people ashore waiting to greet friends. Then the assurance came to me that one group looked like Christians: I waved, they responded and sure enough they were brethren from Marseilles! Here again was 'a stitch in time' of God's Golden Thread — in fact, several stitches and all perfectly timed. My telegram had reached the Junod home in her absence, since she was due to arrive in France on the same day as ourselves, but her friends cabled her ship and received her reply 'Go to meet her.' We were therefore marvellously enabled by the brethren to join the train for the Hague which left only a short time later.

The long train journey of twenty-four hours was a sore trial to the sick one for she had suffered a haemorrhage the night before we landed at Marseilles but we were carried through and were considerably cheered by being met in Paris by Mlle. Junod, who by now had just reached her destination from America. At last, through the 'goodness and mercy' which had followed us over land and sea across the world and sorted out so many problems, some in advance, some seemingly in arrears, but all perfectly timed, we found ourselves in the home of brother Johannes Voorhoeve, father of our missionary Heleen, who has for so many years done so much for our missionary schools in Egypt. The sick nurse was taken to a hospital in the Hague and lived until the following spring when the Lord called her to Himself.

A Break in the Thread?

Before travelling back to England and home, I went to South Germany to visit the family of our mission doctor, Hans Neuffer, whose home was near Stuttgart and, this pleasant duty of contact and first-hand reporting done, I returned to my home looking thin and worn with the long months of responsibility. A thorough medical examination revealed that all was well though the doctor declared it nothing short of miraculous that I should be totally clear of the then dreaded tuberculosis after being so long in close contact with the disease in tropical climates.

But the reader may well be surprised, as indeed I also was at times, that the first three and a half years of a thoroughly prepared and 'prayed about' missionary career should be so consistently and inescapably tied to a sick servant who had to be brought home to die. Is not the lesson to be learned, often at length, that God's guidance for Christian service is invariably tied with a comparatively mundane 'duty'? In other words, God's promise 'I will guide thee with mine eye' (Psalm 32:8) for my spiritual direction is booked in practical detail by His ordering of my circumstances as He says 'I will instruct thee and teach thee in the way which thou shalt go' in the same verse.

In the words of this book we might say that the Golden Thread of God's guidance is to be sought, and found, firmly linked into the basic fabric of circumstances of our every day lives as God's servants.

Chapter 10

Backward, Upward, Forward, Stretch

So sometimes runs the command for preparing the athlete for the coming contest and perhaps it may be used here as some illustration of the spiritual 'gymnastics' which marked my life for the next few months; a period in which I could afterwards see that the Golden Thread had been used to draw together many widely dissimilar strands to form a pattern for a fuller and longer missionary life for me, and that in my beloved China.

Months of uncertainty on my part followed my return to England and certainly the door seemed to close with a bang when in July a letter came from China saying that owing to the civil war there, my school had been forced to close down with apparently little hope of re-opening. Did the Lord wish me to stay on in England and resume my teaching? Almost in the mood of Peter in John 21:3, I felt inclined to pick up the old nets and 'go fishing' again, so in due time I sent for application forms, had an interview with the Education Authority and was on the point of posting off the forms when, going up to London to see Pickering and Inglis about some books I needed, I came face to face with Mr. Harold St. John, who had been a missionary in Brazil and was a very old established friend of mine. In answer to his questions, I explained what I was doing in England and what the situation appeared to be in China, but before I could tell him about my proposed new step to resume teaching, he said, 'Whatever you do, Elsie, remain in the Lord's work.' This I felt to be God's answer to my problem so I went home, tore up the forms and waited.

Soon it became apparent to me that, for the time being at all events, a backward step was required from me. My sister, who helped Father in his business, had been engaged for five years but there seemed no hope of her being free to marry because of an illness which made Father, at that time, very dependent upon her help. Could I step into the gap? I was certainly not so physically strong as she; a life of study had not been conducive to muscular development required for lifting sides of bacon or sacks of rice, but I offered to stay and help Father to set her free. He was glad to accept as he needed the sense of working with someone he knew in order to regain his confidence. Thus I became a shop assistant again and my sister married in March, 1928, and went to live at Iver Heath in Buckinghamshire.

My very inadequacy for the task in the business helped my father to regain the confidence he had lost as the result of a stroke. As he came to help me in lifting weights, he regained his strength and as we also engaged a young girl, buxom and strong, to learn the work, I was free at times to fulfill speaking engagements; so I liked the work. When I took up the shop work, I wrote to the brethren responsible for the support of those in full-time service for the Lord, telling them I was no longer in need of financial help.

After three months, late in June, I was completely taken by surprise one morning when Father came to me and said quite suddenly, 'Look, Elsie, I feel it is not right that I should keep you tied to the shop. I think I can manage now.' This sudden release came like 'a bolt from the blue' and was totally unexpected as I had been prepared to carry on for much longer.

What was I to do now that my 'backward step' had been stopped with a sudden 'halt'? I could hardly write to my friends for funds as a servant of the Lord, and the Lord had shown me that I was not to resume teaching: so I looked upward as I took to my knees in prayer, asking what He wanted me to do next. The answer came this time very speedily, in fact the same day, in the form of a cheque from the brother administering the funds; one who certainly could have had no inkling of what my father was going to say that morning. Thus the Lord put me forth again on the path of faith in service for Him.

An Odd Proposal of Marriage

After a few days of clearing up, I went to Iver Heath for a week's holiday, staying with my married sister, and at the end of that week I received one of the most important letters of my life. It was from Germany, written in that pointed script style which I could hardly read and its import? Could it be true? A proposal of marriage to Mr. Wilhelm Koll whom I had learned to know on the mission field in China. He was now on furlough in Europe but was about to return to China. I dared not discuss the matter with anyone at first for I could not be sure I had read the letter aright; but later, having satisfied myself that my interpretation of the message was correct, I took a long walk in the woods to get alone with God. It will be somewhat difficult for my readers to understand that this matter was not just a question of the heart, for the proposal had been made through a second person rather on the pattern of the Chinese middleman method and, although I had learned to know Mr. Koll on the mission station, the contact had not been such as to prepare me in any way for these circumstances, especially bearing in mind that Chinese etiquette and moral standards did not permit of any familiarity or personal contact between a single man and a single woman.

As I felt myself quite unable to make any clear decision, I resolved to go to Germany to speak with the person who had written the letter; and on arrival in Stuttgart we discussed the whole situation from all possible aspects, the more urgently as it was then discovered that Mr. Koll had now received a call to return to China rather suddenly. Still I lacked any clear guidance for the step I was being invited to take; one which involved so many important consequences such as becoming a wife, and perhaps a mother, in a place where there would be no other Europeans and where perhaps there would be no doctor or other medical advice available. For such a step I felt I should have a definite Word from the Lord, a Word on which I could stand as a rock for the rest of my life, and I did not seem to get it.

During these days I did not ever see Mr. Koll, for he was quite a long distance away in an entirely different part of Germany. When the friends around pressed me for an answer, I could only say that at the present juncture it must only be negative as the Word I needed for such a far-reaching decision had not been given. Meanwhile I was praying that if God wished me to give a different answer He would arrange for me to meet Mr. Koll before he left for China.

Most Odd Answers

So in a few weeks time, missionary Wilhelm Koll left Europe for China and I was left in Stuttgart where I decided to do something useful to earn my living by taking a course in children's nursing at a fine hospital just outside the town. Every help was offered me by way of training, a fortnight in each department involving complete care of babies up to eighteen months old, then with the one to two year olds, and thereafter duty in the milk-kitchen where hundreds of bottles for feeding were prepared each day in a great variety of content consistencies needed to suit the many kinds of sick as well as healthy babies. In retrospect, I saw that this was a great and wonderful preparation for my future needs.

On one of my free days, I visited some of my friends in Stuttgart and was greeted with 'Guess who was here the other day.' My heart gave a great leap but I waited for them to tell me. 'Mr. Koll,' they said, 'but he is now in Italy on the way to China.' So my prayer was answered with a resounding 'NO' — for the time being at least, and I returned to my work among the babies. Where was this Golden Thread? This experience in Germany I find difficult to write about, even after the lapse of so many years; but such are some of the episodes of life down here, especially, it would seem, in the path of service for the Master.

While in Stuttgart, I felt it a good thing to enter for a course in the Missionary School of Medicine at the Homoeopathic Hospital in London due to begin in September that year. The time at the M.S.M. was a great blessing. We had a keen set of students, many of whom have since done great work in China, Thailand, the Philippines and in Guyana where our missionary, Mr. W. H. Sewell, has worked for over forty years.* What I learned there served me through many a crisis in China and was of particular value to me during the illnesses of my own children when there was no qualified doctor around for hundreds of miles.

Slowly in my heart, at this period, there was growing the conviction that one day I should go to China to marry Wilhelm Koll; but how? My feelings are perhaps best illustrated by the following exchanges I remember

---
*This veteran British missionary was called into the Lord's presence September 30, 1980, at Georgetown, Guyana. Aged 85, he served his Lord for over 50 years in the country he loved best.

having with my friend, a fellow student when she said to me, 'Do you love him?' to which I replied, 'I really do not know, everything is so confused.' 'Well, put it this way, if he married someone else, would you mind?' 'Oh, yes, I should be broken hearted,' I replied. 'Well, then, it is quite clear.' 'Yes, perhaps, but what can I do? — I am a woman, and I know him well enough to be sure he will never ask again.' So we decided to pray about it.

That same evening when I arrived home at my lodgings, I was told there was a gentleman waiting to see me. It was, to my surprise, Mr. Mason Roberts, a brother from Leicester who had never before paid me a visit although I knew him very well. After some conversation as to what I was doing and whether I had plans for returning to China which led me to explain the difficulty regarding closure of the school and like matters, he suddenly said, 'Why do you not go out and marry that lonely man, Mr. Koll?' He knew nothing of the proposal I had received and all that had happened since. Was God already answering the united prayer of my friend and myself on the way home from school that day? Then the whole story came out and I explained the problems as I saw them. He was very sympathetic but at once thought that in the circumstances I should write to China although he agreed it was not really the place of a woman to do this. After prayer together, he left me while I begged him not to do anything in the matter and to keep it all very confidential.

Unwomanly Conduct?

The weekend passed very quietly but my meditations led me to seek an interview with my former Bible Class teacher, Mrs. Maxwell-Smith, who had been my greatest spiritual helper in my early years. In those days of one-day postal services, we exchanged postcards and I knew I might visit her on Tuesday evening.

During the afternoon of that day, however, there

came a significant Golden Thread interlude. I was on ward duty at M.S.M. between 4 p.m. and 6 p.m. and as I was feeding a sick child, Mr. C. Granville Hey, the gynaecologist and our lecturer in surgery, and a personal friend of mine (known to a wide circle of brethren simply as 'The Doctor') made his round of the wards. He came up to me and said, 'What a pity you did not marry one of those nice Chinese: you could by now have been feeding one of your own children!' I nearly dropped the spoon for he could know nothing of the problem currently exercising my mind and heart, but my simple reply was, 'I might even do better than that.' He gave me a searching look and said, 'Whatever is afoot, let the choice rest with God.'

After duty, I set off for Streatham and Mrs. Maxwell-Smith. Although I found her sick in bed, she listened attentively to my story and then exclaimed, 'Now I know why God has been saying to me all day that the word for you is from Esther 5, verses 1 and 2.* I could not see how this scripture could possibly fit you, but now I understand. Esther had to do an unwomanly thing in order to bring salvation to others — and you will have to write to Wilhelm in order to be able to go back to China.' Then we sealed the matter with prayer and I left for home to face the most difficult task.

The letter was written and I felt free to plead the parable of the two sons, one who told his father he would go but he did not, and the other who said he would not but he did. With much fear and trembling, I sealed and addressed the envelope ready for posting the next morning and then, but not till then, God gave me the rock-Word for which I had been searching, the Word which has been my plea in every problem assailing me in our 41 years of happy married life. The calendar text was Isaiah 45:2, 'I will go before thee, and

---

* 'Esther put on her royal apparel and stood in the inner court . . . When the king saw Esther . . . the king held out the golden sceptre . . . So Esther drew near and touched the top of the sceptre.' Esther 5:1-2.

make the crooked places straight.' All through the years I have always gone to the Lord claiming this promise and He has never let me down; even in the extremely difficult last year of my dear one's illness until he was taken Home in September, 1971.

The letter, which had been the product of so much careful exercise and looking for direction, was received by a Mr. Koll undoubtedly prepared by the same gracious Master directing my unusual course, and we were engaged by cablegram at the end of the year, 1928, under the key-Word 'Emmanuel' which bound us up together with God for the rest of his pilgrim journey. Moreover the reason for my inability to see clearly earlier, resulting in all the hesitancy described, was made plain, when later, Wilhelm told me how good and necessary he felt it had been to have had that year alone to get back into the Chinese life and language before we started our new life together. And so, it seems to me, the Golden Thread 'tacked me down' for this period to provide for an orderly and efficient restart of work which had been suspended at Hinghwa.

Wedding without Bells in Shanghai

In April, 1929, I finished my course at the Missionary School of Medicine and went to Germany to become acquainted with my fiancé's family and to work in the house of my friend's sister to learn something of German housekeeping and cookery. Then in August, my second journey to China started through Switzerland to Italy whence I sailed from Genoa via Suez, Colombo, Penang, Sumatra and Formosa to Shanghai. Wilhelm was there to meet me and we both stayed in the International Missionary Home. That I was back in the Orient was quickly underlined for me when the hostess, a dear Christian lady, whispered that I must always use the staircase at the opposite end of the house to that used by Wilhelm in order to observe all the Chinese etiquette considered proper for unmarried people. We had to wait two weeks before the marriage could take place, while our names were registered at the appropriate Embassies. There could be no special friends at the wedding because, as I had been informed on board ship on the way out, Mrs. Willis, Senior, had just passed away in South China, which demanded the attention of our dear friends, the Willis family.

So, on October 7th, Wilhelm and I slipped out in rickshaws to the German Embassy and were married with only two unknown clerks from the Embassy to sign the register as witnesses. As it was pouring with rain, I did not even wear the special dress I had bought for the occasion but the day was *ours* and neither of us felt that we had missed anything! A few days later, we left Shanghai to make the long journey up country to reach Hinghwa and a really great welcome by the Chinese brethren. And so, having left China so sadly but with a sense of its being my irrefutable duty to God and man, here I was as surely brought back to the service laid upon my heart, and this time by ways and means as unexpected and unconventional as any I had heard of; but then has He not said, 'My thoughts are not your thoughts, neither are your ways my ways' (Isaiah 55:8) — for me He had shown His ways and thoughts to be heavens higher than the best intentioned earthly planning; a Golden Thread guidance indeed.

Chapter 11

Seven Years of Peace and Profit

The Lord now granted us a new start to a seven-year period of peaceful service undisturbed by any serious alarms of war or riots. The school was soon opened again at the request of the Chinese brethren and we started at the East Gate house where I had lived and worked during my first term of service, but now we made our home in the flat at the top of the hospital building, formerly occupied by Dr. Neuffer and his family, the very place in which my hasty farewell party had been held more than two years earlier. The hospital itself had been closed when Dr. Neuffer had been obliged to return to Germany. He had not been able to come back and although the hospital was on two occasions re-opened for short periods by a Chinese worker, there seemed no possibility of it succeeding on a permanent basis. At this time, also, Mr. and Mrs. Ruck decided to settle in Peking and I was able therefore to take over more accommodation as extra classrooms for the school in the East Gate house.

The school enjoyed a rapid growth; a former teacher, daughter of the converted opium smoker, Mr. Li, was able to return although she was by then married to Dr. Rong (a former pupil of Dr. Neuffer from whom he had received some initial medical training), and in addition, we had another dear girl, Miss Wang, daughter of a high local official, who had earlier been won for the Lord. Then also the Lord permitted us to see some fruit from the original school started when I first began work at Hinghwa, of which the following is an example.

Precious Fragrance

Not the name of an exotic eastern perfume, nor yet of an exquisite spiritual exercise or experience, but the English translation of Pao Hsien, the Chinese name of one of my first pupils, then a wee mite of seven years — who later, in the Lord's goodness, lived up to her name.

During my absence in England, she had been working in a silk factory run by the Japanese who were in the habit of employing such young children to snatch the silk cocoons from boiling water so that while hot they could be drawn out in long threads for spinning. It was a very hard life for the little ones, working from early morning until late at night under very poor conditions for shockingly meagre pay. Shortly after our school re-opened, the mother of Precious Fragrance came back to Hinghwa and the girl was presented to the home of her aunt whose son she was later destined to marry. This was a common practice with poor girls whose parents could not afford to keep them. After the engagement, the child would go into the home of her future mother-in-law and become the little drudge of the family until the time came to be married.

For Precious Fragrance, this was by no means an easy life but it gave her the chance to come to Sunday School, only, however, under the forbidding condition that she must not 'eat Jesus,' their term for becoming a believer. The first thing this little one learned by heart in my first school was the 23rd Psalm, which in time was fulfilled in her own life, for the Lord became her Shepherd. With her finding of the Saviour came the desire to win others, so she attended our Wednesday women's prayer meeting and began to pray for her cousin, the sister of her fiancé. At first, the mother-in-law would not let this girl, her own daughter, come to Sunday School; but in time, Precious Fragrance persuaded her that the cousin could make a better marriage if she had 'swallowed some characters,' that is, learned to read, so she was allowed to come to the day school but with strict orders 'not to believe!' God has His way sometimes in the midst of the storm and also at times in the fire.

Baptism Through Fire

It was about the time of the harvest moon when it was the custom for each home to prepare a table in the courtyard spread with cakes and fruit for the Queen of Heaven as a thank-offering for the gathered crops. The mother-in-law of Precious Fragrance was busy baking her cakes in the usual type of clay oven fired by straw; the method of operation being to stuff great bundles of straw or dried river reeds into the grate, drag them out again when the pot boils and stamp them out with the feet to extinguish the flames. In the midst of her cooking, the good woman heard someone scrambling around on the thatched roof of the hut and rushed out to scold some boys who were trying to rescue their kite entangled in the thatch. Alas! The stove straw was still aglow and in a few seconds the whole of the straw fuel and the mud house were in flames.

Little could be saved, as in such a place, the luxury of a proper fire brigade did not exist. In case of fire, a gong sounded to summon men from all quarters in town and field to form chain systems to pass water buckets from hand to hand — but invariably by the time these were organised and water had been located, bearing in mind there was no mains water supply, all was lost; as we say today, 'too little, too late!' But in idol-ridden China, fire was laid at the door of the 'fox-god' because of the association with his reddish hair. He was, therefore, an object of worship to be suitably placated and it followed that the blame for such a fire, as we have described, fell upon the victim since surely he must have neglected these necessary honours.

Now on this basis, no one would take the destitute occupants of a burnt house into his own home lest he, too, should offend the fire god with the all too frequent result that such a family must often spend days on the street without shelter. So Precious Fragrance came along to ask if I would take them in. Now here was a real test; for Mr. Koll was away on a preaching itinerary and I was alone with two children, added to which, if I had a phobia, it was regarding 'fire.' But God gave strength: I took them all in, accepting the responsibility, and witnessed the never failing truth that 'deeds speak louder than words' — for the Lord used this incident to lead the much-prayed-for cousin to Himself.

At the Chinese New Year when we had a conference, there was usually a time for baptism. Both Precious Fragrance and her cousin wished to be baptised but mother-in-law said firmly that if they became Christians, she would turn them both out of her home. They were, nonetheless, very determined and hid their change of garments in my house, were both baptised and then jointly witnessed at home that this had taken place. Behold! They were not turned out, and when later in conversation with the mother, I asked why she had not put her threat into action, she replied, 'Well, they are really better girls than most around here, so I didn't.'

Such specimens of the work in time of political peace and the seeming quiet of 'everyday life' serve, however, to remind us that the enemy has his fiery agents seeking to hinder the Gospel blessing but that our Master of every tempest is more than a match for his frightening 'fire gods' even where these are believed in by some.

Chapter 12

Childbirth in China plus Travel

In October, 1930, we had the joy of receiving our first baby, our little daughter, Ruth. My missionary friend, Mrs. Ruck, of Peking, was also expecting a little one a few weeks later and we had, therefore, decided to go to Peking for the birth and, for this purpose, had hired a boat to take us down to the junction with the big River Yangtse early in September. But when the day arrived and we were standing all ready and packed for the long journey, a messenger came to tell us that our boat had been seized by bandits. This meant that we had to take a passage on the 'Treasure Boat,' a means of public transport which carried businessmen and cash down the river. This was not very easy for me as one had to sit quite still on the hard wooden bench among a group composed entirely of men on the vessel which completely lacked toilet facilities. Expectant mothers, past and present, will at once appreciate what this meant.

When eventually we reached Shanghai in safety, it was to find that there was no room in the Missionary Home, but 'Golden Thread memories' were evoked when the kind hostess, who had looked after me when we were married, recognised me, observed my need and gave me a bed on her verandah and allowed Mr. Koll to sleep on the floor in the dining room. Next we discovered that a miniature civil war was in progress along the main railway line to Peking so our journey must be by ship on the East China Sea, a trip of three and a half days duration, if one could get tickets which were in high demand. My husband had to return to the Missionary Home, find me and take me down to the Chinese Shipping Office before we could persuade them that the urgency of the situation warranted a booking. But after the sea trip and another train journey of several hours, we arrived in the capital and our little daughter was born in the German Hospital there on the 3rd of October.

Ring for Service

While I was in the hospital, my husband, accompanied by Mr. Ruck, paid a visit to his brother, Gustav Koll and his wife, Lili, who then worked in our mission station in North China. Opportunity for this contact also meant that it was not until Ruth was a month old that we had to begin the long trek home starting with the train journey to Tientsin, the big port, whence we would take the steamer down to Shanghai, finishing with a reverse of the river trip mentioned at the beginning of the chapter.

Conditions were more comfortable for me (or I was better able to face them) but care of the baby was our priority. We were not in the times or at the place for acquiring 'karricots' or 'Moses baskets' as used for modern child comfort in travel so I bought an old-fashioned Japanese basket in which I was able to fit a horse-hair mattress and curtains of white net. When not needed by the baby, it carried all the gear; when needed as a cot, one turned up the deep lid on end at the head of the basket and the white net curtains and ribbon draperies completed the facility for the small traveller.

This proved most convenient for boat or train but on the Peking to Tientsin express, it led to more attentive service than we had anticipated. A steward paid me visit after visit, sure that I had rung the service bell — until we discovered that the mobile cot-cum-Japanese-basket was resting on the bell-push! All things considered, we were most thankful and very glad when the long journey home was over and our little one safely settled in her home routine.

In Perils of Waters

In Mid-1931, when our baby was about nine months old, our district which lay below sea level suddenly became a 'disaster area.' One evening we retired to bed after a last look from the verandah at the pleasant vista of ripening rice stretching away to the horizon, to awake the next morning to a devastating scene, in which the promising harvest was replaced by a vast waste of water, broken only by a solitary tree-top or cottage roof sticking up here and there. The dams had burst higher up the canal and the swirling waters had even penetrated the city streets in spite of the high walls. Friends had to take boats to come to the assembly meetings. At our street door we had to place straw barricades to keep out floating rubbish including such hazards to health as dead rats and cats.

It was almost five months before life began to resume normal proportions and this period brought much additional work and responsibility for my husband, who was appointed the local representative for the International Famine Relief Organisation. As the waters were first drained out from inside the city, thousands of refugees fled into it. They slept in temples or any other public places. Presently great bundles of used clothing sent by other Chinese in Hong Kong and Singapore filled the bottom storey of our house. Great rice-kitchens were set up in the city, Mr. Ruck and a group of Salvation Army officers came down from Peking to help in the distribution. As there was no registration of birth and death, it was very difficult to issue food tickets, and the only time to count the number of heads in a family was for Mr. Koll and the other helpers to go out about 2 a.m., wading knee deep in water, to count them in bed.

For nearly five months, thousands were fed in the city. Then there were the others out in the country, who had no boats to come to the city, living in the tree tops or on the roof. To help these, outboard motors were attached to ordinary houseboats and some of the officers would go out daily with loads of pre-baked biscuits or pancake-like bread, because it was useless to give rice as they had no dry fuel to cook with. All this upheaval led to a problem with our little one, as we could get no powdered milk from Shanghai (the Chinese do not drink milk). Then there was infection everywhere as is always the case in such national disasters, so she developed infant diarrhea. One of the S.A. officers said to me, 'Why do you not try goat's milk?' I had never seen a goat in Hinghwa, but he told me that he had seen a goat with two kids at the city gate just brought in by some refugees. We immediately set about negotiating and, for about twelve and sixpence, we bought the goat and her kids which saved the life of little Ruth.

From that time, we kept nanny goats to get a little milk each day; it is always T.B. free and, if one does not keep the male with them, there is none of the strong smell usually associated with goat's milk. When we needed more kids, we sent them to the other side of the city where we later found a Mohammedan, who kept goats as his religion did not allow him to eat pork, which was the only meat one could obtain in Hinghwa.

The flood brought me one new opportunity in that some of the older girls, children of our country

Christians, who normally had no time to come to school, came with their folk to take refuge in our house. The top floor housed our family and the foreign helpers; the next floor made a home for many of the Christians from the outlying country districts. Although it was a busy time for us all, I felt we must use this opportunity and began to teach these country girls to read. This was especially a help to the grandchildren of old sister Han. One of these girls to whom we gave the name of Ai Deh, which means 'obtaining love,' became the Christian wife of the fourth brother of the Chieh family from the 'White-Foal' village, one of our out-stations.

The flood also brought some interesting episodes. One day we heard a plane, the first ever seen in Hinghwa. We rushed out on to the verandah to look, and there was a seaplane settled on the water at a distance from the city wall, while hundreds of tiny houseboats were hurrying out to reach it. Mr. Ruck, and another of officer, tried to get a boat to go out and investigate, but all available boats had gone to the place. Presently we saw the plane take off and fly away. They had had to leave because the little boats, hoping to get some help, crowded near the wings of the plane and the open-air cooking stoves on the boats threatened a fire danger for the plane.

Twenty-four hours later, my husband received a telegram from the government in Nanking asking us to receive Charles Lindbergh, but the message had come a day too late. When the five-month famine relief work was coming to an end, Mr. Koll sent me to the nearest American Mission Station to get a few days rest (by 'near' we mean a journey of at least 24 hours in a Chinese houseboat). During my absence, the 'Red Dean' of Canterbury accompanied by some American missionaries came to inspect the flood conditions and stayed the night at our home. When I asked my husband later what he had given them to eat, he replied, 'Corned beef and fried potatoes! After all, he came to see flood conditions.'

Just towards the end of this period, we heard a rumour that the government was coming round to seize all empty hospital buildings to set up some clinics. Now, as we were living there and also had all the assembly meetings there, we did not wish to be occupied. Hitherto I had still been holding my school in the East Gate house, built by Mr. Hutton, the father of Mrs. Ruck and the pioneer missionary of our town.

After quick consultation, we decided that the best thing would be to turn our hospital building overnight into a school. But how? We couldn't transport the desks and blackboards through the streets which were still not quite returned to normal conditions. So we hired boats, loaded up all the school equipment, poled the boats outside the city till they reached a spot behind the hospital and dragged it all up with ropes, piece by piece, over the city wall. Meanwhile we prepared rooms, put away all the hospital apparatus which had not been used since Dr. Neuffer's time in China. Lo and behold; by the next morning, there was a fully furnished school and notices were put up on the city gates to announce the re-opening of the school which had had to close while we were under water. So from that time, the school was held in our own building, which greatly facilitated matters when I later had to teach my own children as well as run the Chinese School.

Chapter 13

Arrival
of Another Baby

In the Autumn of 1932, we were expecting another happy event, the birth of a second little one. After the experience of the arduous journey to Peking for the birth of Ruth, we decided to go to the nearest American missionary hospital for the arrival. Thus arrangements were made with the doctor in Taichow to come to them towards the end of November. For this, too, a journey of twenty-four hours on a Chinese houseboat, was necessary. On the afternoon of November 2nd was my Wednesday women's meeting, and as we closed at 5 o'clock, my Chinese teacher from the school came up to me and said, 'Do you know that you are going to get your baby this evening?' 'No, that cannot be, it is not due for another fortnight,' was my reply. But she pointed out several symptoms which she had noticed while I was busy taking the class, and I, too, began to realise that the possibility was there. I hastened upstairs to warn my husband of what was to happen.

It was a shock, because both of us had only a very slight knowledge of midwifery and neither of us had done a birth. However, he set to work to sterilise what was necessary, while I went to the kitchen to tell the women to get as much hot water ready as possible. By this time, it was 6 o'clock and I had had to give in, so I laid down on the hard bed which I had hastily prepared with the midwifery book beside me and an earnest prayer to my heavenly Father that no complications might arise for I knew how anxious my dear husband was.

All went well and by 8 o'clock, we had a healthy little son. My dear Chinese teacher came to bathe the baby as she had learned our ideas of hygiene and Mr. Koll was too busy looking after me. Also, I might mention that there had been very little privacy; the dear Chinese friends were keen to see how foreigners would behave under such difficult circumstances. Many months later, one of the sisters said to me, 'we asked how you behaved, and I felt very ashamed when I heard how you had taken it.'

Excitement Over Birth

The triumph of the local Christians was great, for they declared that for the birth of the first baby I had gone to a big foreign hospital and had only had a daughter, whereas now by remaining in their city, I had had a son! The excitement did not end when he had safely arrived. The custom on the birth of a son is to buy a big stock of duck's eggs, boil them hard in a copper tub of red dye, and distribute baskets of them to all your lady friends in the hope that it will bring them a son in the near future. Thus all attention was placed on the egg market and the dyeing pot, while Mr. Koll was left to look after me and the baby, with the result that he had a new patient the next night, as he had Ruth sick because the kind friends had been feeding her on hard boiled duck's eggs.

When Godfrey was one month old, we had to make a big feast for all the local assembly, including the nearest Christian farming community. The entertainment started early in the day when all were served with elaborately prepared noodles with ham, etc. (noodles

Elsie and Wilhelm Koll with Ruth and Godfrey, circa 1933/34

Elsie Koll with Chinese Old Girls' Association
to which she taught baby care

are always eaten on birthdays because the long strings which one must get into the mouth as daintily as possible without breaking them should represent long life wishes). After this noodle breakfast, the guests amused themselves until the big feast later in the day. I do not remember exactly how many sat down but it was at least forty guests. Godfrey was presented with a proper baby boy's outfit in beautiful silk, a crimson jacket, an apple-green waistcoat, royal blue trousers and a gorgeous cap, like a crown with no top with hanging chain ornaments of different charms, each of which represented some special wish for his future.

In the meantime, we were able to settle down to normal life again. The big problem when Ruth was a baby was that I had not been able to completely breast-feed her. Now that we had some goats, I sent word to the doctor in Taichow telling him that the baby had already arrived and asking for the schedule for feeding with goat's milk. My old Chinese helper in the kitchen, however, told me that if I would drink all that she gave me I would be able to nurse him myself, so I agreed to try without always asking what the ingredients were. The result was I could nurse Godfrey right through the next hot season, seven months without using any schedule, which is a great asset in a country where there is a temperature of over 80°F and no possible chance of refrigeration. It was also his salvation when he developed whooping cough at a time when my husband was away from home, and I had no other help. After every bout of coughing, when I had removed the phlegm from his throat, I fed him and in this way he did not lose weight and get weak; he was then only four to five months old.

Chapter 14

Hygiene Lessens Child Mortality

During this period of school work, we started the Old Girls' Association, which soon numbered about 150 members. They could not all come at once, but we had a meeting once a month. As most people had no reliable clocks and paid little heed to the calendar, we sent out a message on the day of the proposed gathering. In the first session, I had hygiene and infant care lessons, so necessary as many of the girls were already married. Practical demonstration was given by using a big doll.

Infant mortality had always been great. If the mother died or had no milk, there was no substitute except rice water, as there was no milk or milk powder, for the Chinese of our province neither drank milk nor ate any of its products. One of the results of the hygiene instruction was seen in the remark of the mother-in-law of the teacher who had married the young Christian, Dr. Rong, a former pupil of our mission surgeon, Dr. Neuffer; 'Alas,' sighed the old lady, 'I had eight children, but at least half of them died; what shall we do now to support all these grandchildren if they all stay alive as a result of all this hygiene?'

About this time, an old sister in Holland, who was due to have the big birthday party usual on one's eightieth birthday, decided to forego it and gave the money to buy me an epidiascope projector for my school. With it one could show either slides or any pictures. I could even project the full page of our Chinese hymn-book. Another dear friend in America, Mr. G. A. Kaschel, had paid the contribution each year for the National Geographic Magazine for the use of my own children. Mr. Koll took all the pictures from back numbers and filed them according to the country of origin, so I was able to follow up the infant-care course with lantern lectures on different parts of the world. This meant a great deal in a place where there was little public entertainment. After the lectures, we always had an epilogue so that we could keep them in touch with God's Word. Thus work went on quietly until 1936.

During those years, we had been able to get away to the mountains once or twice to escape the hot, humid monsoon air of the plains. There we were able to meet Mrs. Ruck and members of her family. In the autumn of 1936, we went to Shanghai to meet Gustav and Lili Koll on their return from Europe with Siegfried, their adopted Chinese boy. At the same time, we could make some purchases of foreign clothes ready for our furlough in the following year. On the mission station, we almost always wore Chinese clothes and ate Chinese food.

Chapter 15

War Shadows in Europe

L ittle did we guess all that would happen in the next two years, when we set out in the spring of 1937 to return to England, where my children would see Grandma and their other relations for the first time. My father never saw the children as he was called Home in 1936. Soon after we left China, the Sino-Japanese war broke out, and when we landed in England, we received the news that Hitler had closed all our meeting rooms in Germany. After months of happy fellowship in England, we went to my husband's home in Barmen-Elberfeld in May, 1938. As we did not feel free to sign the paper agreeing to Hitler's politics and so did not join 'the Bund,' we used to visit forbidden groups each Sunday in private houses, where my husband usually spoke at the meeting. This continued as we moved from place to place until August, when Mr. Koll went to visit the assemblies in Switzerland, while I paid a visit to my dear friend and colleague of China, Ruth Neuffer, who was then married and living in Trier on the Moselle.

While we were there, Godfrey fell ill with symptoms very like pneumonia; he was so bad that the doctor advised us to send for his father. Our little son was spared to us but the doctor advised us not to proceed at

once to England but to take a rest in the Black Forest.
Now arose the question, 'Where?' In the Black Forest
was one assembly still 'Breaking Bread.' Should we go
to this place and share the danger of arrest as we had
hitherto done each Sunday? After prayer, we each came
separately to the conclusion that we should go
elsewhere. On that very first Sunday of our holiday, the
Gestapo arrested the brethren of that meeting. Here the
Golden Thread had appeared in a very special way, for
had we been there we should have lost our passports
and perhaps never been able to return to China again.

England and Germany at War

With this experience, my husband decided that he
should return to China at once, although he felt that I
should remain with the children in England until the
fighting with the Japanese had cleared in our district. So
we went back to England and by the time of the Munich
Conference, Wilhelm was on his way back to China on
board an Italian steamer. For me, the time seemed to
pass very slowly, while the children attended the village
school in Iver Heath in Buckinghamshire where my
mother and sister lived.

In the spring of 1939, I booked passages on a North-
German-Lloyd steamer to return to China in August.
Everything was packed and crated by the end of July
and, on August 1st, the children had a little farewell
party for their school friends. The next day Ruth was
feverish, and when the doctor came, he diagnosed
'Scarlet Fever,' which meant, at that time in England,
one month in isolation hospital, where she was taken by
ambulance on August 3rd. Where now was the Golden
Thread?

We lost our passage on the boat due on August 26th —
only the very necessary clothes had been left out for us.
Winter things were all in the crated boxes. Ruth was
allowed home on September 2nd and at 11 o'clock on

Transport by wheel-barrow, circa 1936.
Elsie Koll, Ruth and Godfrey and hired man

Elsie and Wilhelm Koll with Ruth and Godfrey, 1938

the morning of September 3rd, war with Germany was declared. That evening the police came to see where my husband was, and were very relieved to find that he was in China and need not be interned. Meanwhile I was forbidden to go more than 3 miles out of the village except to register with the police in Slough once a week, for I too had a German passport.

The next few months passed for me as if one were going through a long dark tunnel, so long that one cannot see a glimmer of light from the other end. No news came from China: Should I ever get back to my loved one? On November 7th, I was called before the Aliens' Tribunal in Slough. When the judge glanced through the letters of reference which I had received from many of the leading brethren, he pounced on one from Mr. Granville Hey, the surgeon from the London Homoepathic Hospital, and asked me if he were a friend of mine. When I affirmed this, he asked me if my husband was anti-British. My reply was that had he been so, he would hardly have married me. After a short pause, the judge said, 'Mrs. Koll, I will set you free and may God bless you and take you safely back to your work in China.' At once I began negotiating for a ship's passage, which was not very easy. My German passport did not allow me to go via Suez because permission was refused by France. Canada did not want me. At last, the American Consul gave permission to travel over America, provided I first took my trans-Pacific ticket.

Chapter 16

At Sea
Under Wartime
Black-Out

On January 26th, 1940, we began the sea journey. The preceding fortnight had seen the sinking of three great liners torpedoed by the German submarines off the English coast. No one was allowed to know the name of the ship I would sail on. The amount of money each passenger was allowed to take was very small. After staying the night with the dear family White of Birkenhead, I was allowed no friend to go with me on the dock, although Mrs. White came as far as ever she was allowed, but from the moment I took the first lonely step into the waiting room, packed with European refugees from Hitler, the good Hand of my God was upon me. As I stood waiting with Ruth and Godfrey at the end of the hall, a senior officer from the ship passed through the corridor, and called to me. 'You do not belong to that crowd of refugees.' I explained about my German passport but he waived it and bid me follow him. Almost at once we were on the ship and given a cabin a little higher up in the boat.

Twelve long days followed in a ship completely blacked out, zigzagging all the time to dodge submarines. We were never fully undressed at night, I carried all my papers in a water-proof bag round my neck, and three life-belts wherever we went. At last we arrived in Halifax in Canada, where it was bitterly cold, an ice blue coast, and a cutting wind. Then I asked the captain if I might send a telegram to one of the friends in New York so as to get some help on arrival, as I had never been to America before. The captain said he could not allow it as we still faced danger all along the coast. So I had to wait and stay upon my God.

As we approached the dock in New York, I stood with much trepidation waiting to disembark. Just then the purser called out, 'Is there a Mrs. Koll on board?' There was a Captain Barlow, a dear Christian, and one of the chief officers of the Cunard Line, awaiting me. He explained that he had heard from some missionaries in England, that some time a Mrs. Koll with two children would arrive, so he had made enquiries as each boat came in. Off went Ruth and Godfrey with his steward to wait in a warm office. Meanwhile in a very short time, my whole 17 pieces of luggage had passed the customs under the help of Captain Barlow. When I explained that I had not been allowed to contact our Christian friends in New York about our arrival, he was about to lead me off to his office to wait until he had finished the rest of his duties on the ship, when someone tapped me on the shoulder, saying, 'Are you Mrs. Koll?'

It was Mr. Kaschel of Paterson, New Jersey, who had also heard that I might arrive one day, and so had come to the dock as each ship came in and had waited by the Letter 'K' at the customs. After thanking Captain Barlow very much for his kindness and collecting the children, we were taken to Mr. Kaschel's home.

Over Land by Rail

When I told him the time I was due to join my boat in San Francisco on the President Line, he said it was not possible to get there in time, for our Atlantic trip had taken much longer than usual. Although he gave me a hearty invitation to stay with them in America for a time, I explained how I had given the American Consul in London the assurance that I would only make a transit trip across the U.S.A. So Mr. Kaschel telephoned the President Line to see what could be done. Again the Golden Thread emerged and we were told that my boat had been held up for propeller repairs, so I had plenty of time. When we had obtained the cheap ticket allowed to pastors and missionaries, for the eastern side of America, the railway informed us that the freight luggage would hardly reach San Francisco in time. So the Paterson assembly had a special prayer meeting that evening asking God to take my luggage through in time.

The next evening we took the night express to Chicago, where we were met by brothers Gast and Nehring. As it was snowing hard, the latter took the children off to a warm place, while Mr. Gast and I went to apply for the western half of the cheap ticket. When we presented it at the ticket office, we met with a rebuff. 'No clergyman travels with 17 pieces of luggage and a baby buggy.' (The baby buggy, so called, was a large doll's pram which had been given me for Ruth and which I had stuffed with cushions.) 'Moreover,' said the clerk, 'the luggage will not get through in time.' After a long discussion, Mr. Gast offered to pay for a sleeper, a thing which I had not dared to do considering the small sum of English money which I had been allowed to bring with me, although we were to spend two and a half days and nights on the train. At this, the clerk melted, did some 'phoning,' came back and gave us the ticket, quietly saying at the same time, 'I have just heard that your luggage has already passed Chicago.' That is why God allowed us to be held up at the ticket office that I might be assured that our prayers had already been answered.

That night at 11:00 p.m., after attending the German-speaking prayer meeting of the Chicago assembly, we boarded the 'Trail-Blazer' for San Francisco. After travelling two days through bleak snow-covered landscape, crossing the Salt Lake at Salt Lake City, climbing up the snow-clad trail of the Rocky Mountains, we awoke the next morning to find roses blooming in California. Just before 6:00 a.m., the black steward handed me a telegram telling me to alight at a station called Oaklands and I would be met by a Mr. Zimmermann, the representative of the Seamen's Mission in San Francisco, who had been acquainted with the news of my arrival by the friends in Chicago. On enquiring how far away Oaklands was, I learned that we only had about a quarter of an hour. What a scramble to dress, gather up all the food supplies which had been given me by kind friends in New York to save the expensive meals on the train, and the numerous toys in the shape of a big pink elephant, a Betsy-Wetsy doll, etc., plus two big boxes of chocolates in the shape of hearts, as it had been St. Valentine's day when we boarded the train in Chicago. However, we were ready as the express pulled in at the station to enter on the next stage of our adventures.

Mr. Zimmermann was there to meet us, but as he had duty on the docks that morning, he took us to the home of Dr. Neils Nielson, a veterinary surgeon, where we received a very warm welcome. Here, Godfrey was in his element, for he enjoyed the monkeys and other animals. Mrs. Nielson explained to me that the house had been left to her by her mother on condition that she welcomed any missionaries of any denomination who were in need of accommodation. After a hearty breakfast, we were taken below to a basement floor which was on a level with the garden at the back of the house, and were told that this would be our private apartment. It seemed to be devoid of furniture, but still wondering at its bareness, I thanked her very much, waiting to see what would happen. Presently she began to press buttons in the walls, and out came tables, chairs, beds and bedding, in fact all that one could possibly need. Her next move was to phone the docks to find out about our luggage, and we heard that it had all arrived safely in time. What a God we have who answers prayer!

Peaceful Pacific

As America was not yet involved in the war, we had a peaceful trip across the Pacific. On board, we were to learn the reason for the whole delay in our journeyings. Among the other Christians with whom we were soon able to gather for prayer and reading, was a young Swedish couple, who told me that they had boarded in Hamburg the same ship which we were to have joined in Southampton on August 26th, 1939. The journey had proceeded according to schedule as far as Gibraltar, where Hitler ordered all German ships to return to Germany. For the Swedish missionaries it had not been too difficult, because theirs was a neutral country, but if God had not allowed Ruth to get scarlet fever, we three would have been landed in Germany and obliged to stay there for the rest of the war. How good is the good Hand of our God upon us!

From San Francisco I cabled Mr. Koll that we were on our way. Hitherto I had refrained from doing so because I felt it would spare him the anxiety of thinking about the risky part of the sea voyage. Nor did I know the war conditions in China in our district, so it was doubtful whether he would receive the telegram or not. To our joy, he was able to get down to Shanghai to meet us, but it was a disappointment to find that the fighting on the road was too bad to allow us to go back home with him at once. The kind Willis family offered to lend us part of one of the steel-built houses on their compound, so we settled down to make yet another temporary home.

Two other ladies of the Presbyterian Mission whose

route would partly coincide with that of my husband when he decided to return to Hinghwa, asked if they might travel together. On the way they were held up at pistol point by armed robbers, who took all their valuables including their gold wedding rings. My husband lost his ring too, but he had not anything else of much value except his watch which he always kept covered with an old scratched cellophane shield. When the robbers snatched it, one look decided that it was not worth the taking and so returned it. His money was hidden behind the picture in his passport wallet, so it was not discovered.

After six months spent in the little steel house, we were able to travel up country to our home in Hinghwa. The journey by boat and houseboat was even more difficult than usual, as we were held up at different checkpoints and everything was examined by the Japanese. We were travelling with the Montgomery family who had just returned from America and were bringing new equipment for the hospital in Chinchiang Pu for Dr. Bell, the father-in-law of Billy Graham. It was the examination of all this freight which took so long, but the soldiers amused themselves by turning out Godfrey's model railway equipment and playing with it on the wharf. From my costume, they tore open the corners to extract the tailor's lead weights in case I might be hiding ammunition. But it was all worthwhile to be back home and into the work again. As we had German passports, we were never interned and were able to carry on right up to the time when the Communists came in 1946.

Chapter 17

Japanese Marines
Storm Hinghwa

Already before we arrived from England, Mr. Koll
had experienced one siege by the Japanese army.
They took Hinghwa but occupied it first only for a short
time, and then retreated. Formerly we had a small
electric plant run by some wealthy men in the city and
although there was not much power, we used to get
some light from sunset to midnight, but now the
Japanese destroyed the dynamo and set fire to the dried
egg factory just outside the city wall near our house.
Mr. Koll spent hours on the roof organising a chain of
buckets from inside the hospital to save the building
from catching fire.

When we all arrived in the autumn of 1940, the city
was not occupied but one morning when I was teaching
our children, we heard a plane and rushed to the
verandah to see what for us was an unusual sight. While
we gazed, the plane swerved over the South Gate of the
city, dropped bombs and flew off. Then we realised that
we were to be besieged again.

The next few days were nerve-racking. Most of the
Christian families came to stay with us. During the
bombardment, we all took refuge in the lower corridor
which ran between the rooms which were the wards of

the former hospital and so had no outside walls. One shell hit the city wall just behind the house or it would have gone clean through the house. The worst moment was when the city surrendered and the Japanese marines, with fixed bayonets, stormed into the North Gate just at the end of our road, stabbing most of the refugees who had taken cover in the Buddhist temple at the gate.

As we wanted to protect the fifty-six people who had come to our home, Mr. Koll and I stood at the open door of the hospital with our children standing in front of us, since Godfrey declared he would rather be killed first than see us killed. The soldiers stormed up the street, pushed past us into the house, but the officer called a halt when he read the notice in Chinese declaring that we were German citizens which, by law, we had had to have posted at the main door for some time. After Mr. Koll talked with him, the ordinary soldiers were ordered to leave, while the officer inspected all our refugees who had had to line up inside. When they found no arms and they had examined the house from top to bottom, even looking into the water tanks, the officer withdrew and we were left in peace.

As a result of our kindness in taking in the whole family of Precious Fragrance, another of her prayers were answered in that her second cousin came to the Lord. Life was not easy because there was no more chance of getting stores from the coast whether of food or medicine. We were constantly under surveillence and only left the mission once during the six years of Japanese occupation.

Wartime Shortages

One of the big problems was shortage of funds as none of the European countries could send us gifts except Switzerland through the Red Cross to Mlle. Junod in Nanking. When America entered the war in 1941 after

Pearl Harbour, we saw inflation getting worse, so we took what money we had in hand and bought stocks of unhusked wheat and rice from the corn-market and stored it in the unused rooms in the house, which had once been the hospital. With rice one can pay all the helpers for they preferred it to money which was always losing its value. At the time of the new harvest, wheat in May and rice in September, the stocks of the old harvest sold for more than it had been bought, and we could buy a new supply. It was this that kept us alive as we always could send our own grain to the mill when we needed new flour or rice, and moreover, was more nourishing, containing all the vitamins, as it was not polished. We could also help the brothers who laboured in the Gospel work. We liked Chinese food, so we managed without butter, cheese, jam, milk, etc. From the Chinese goats, we managed to get enough milk for the children. With the flour from our wheat, we baked bread once a week when the fuel became scarce. Sometimes we got a little wild honey brought in by the Christian boatmen from the country assemblies. With plenty of local grown peanuts, we were able to roast, mince, and mix them with lard to make peanut butter.

The Japanese dismantled the electric light works from which we had formerly had a poor light for a few hours each evening. Kerosene soon became very scarce, so we managed with cotton threads as wicks in saucers of peanut oil, except for one hour after supper, when we had a small oil lamp by which I used to read aloud for the children while they knitted to keep their fingers busy, although not much grew from the work as we had so little wool that it had to be continually unpicked and knitted up again.

Coal was unobtainable and later wood became very scarce, as the Japanese used it for charcoal to fire their heating braziers. Thus we could only use the oven once a week, when we baked bread, roasted a kid, did the

ironing and all other such chores. For the rest, I had a
Chinese mud stove built into the kitchen. This was fired
with straw, the long bundles of river reeds which all
Chinese used as fuel. The Japanese did not interfere with
the meetings, although martial law obliged us to arrange
Bible-readings and prayer meetings at 5 o'clock in the
afternoon instead of later in the evenings. For a time I
was able to carry on the Chinese day school but later the
Japanese abolished English as a foreign language subject
in schools and demanded that their own tongue should
be taught. As I wanted to avoid complications for the
future, should the war be over and a normal Chinese
government return to power, I decided to close the day
school rather than teach Japanese, but this gave me a
new opportunity for service. Many of the older teenage
students were keen on continuing their English studies,
so I started a private class for English lessons on the
condition that they used the Gospel of Luke as the main
textbook.

We also continued lessons in composition and
grammar from their old school books. We had a supply
of the Scripture Gift Mission's smaller Gospel books so I
was able to give them all one. God blessed this class and
quite a number of these young men and women were
baptized and received into fellowship before the
Communists took over our city, for by that time the
Sunday Bible class which these young folk chose to
attend, numbered about thirty. In spite of the fact that
the day school was closed, the numbers in the Sunday
School did not diminish. One problem arose about
baptism, because our baptistry was outside the East
Gate of the city and it was dangerous for the older girls
to pass the sentries at the city gate. So when my
daughter, Ruth, and her five Chinese girlfriends were
baptized, it was done in one of the huge earthenware
water pots which stood in our courtyard holding the
water supply. They had to kneel inside but could be
quite immersed.

Chapter 18

Life Under Japanese Occupation

The education of our own children presented quite a problem at this time. After three years of enemy occupation, the supply of English textbooks which I had brought from England in 1940 was exhausted and more advanced ones were unobtainable. The only solution was to switch over to German schoolbooks for all subjects, so again the Golden Thread was visible and one could see, even more clearly than earlier when I married, why it had been directed that I did German at the High School stage instead of chemistry.

Meanwhile, the war dragged on until the surrender of Germany took place. We had no news at all apart from the Chinese newspapers. Rumours of the steady advance of Communist troops kept coming. At that time, they posed as helping the Generalissimo to free the land from the Japanese. Money was very scarce so that I sold my harmonium to some Christians in another town in order to buy flannelette to make new pyjamas for the family. We always wore Chinese clothes, but for underwear, I had already unpicked, washed and re-knitted all the children's outgrown woollies to make vests which turned out to be 'coats of many colours,' for a few inches would be red or pink, followed by strips of yellow or white. Striped curtains were turned into shirts for Godfrey. We also learned how to spin our own cotton thread and make shoe-soles of old rags in case the day came when we could no longer keep any servants; a thing which we wished to avoid as long as possible, because they were our liaison with the troops, especially later when the area was taken over by the Communists.

The process for making shoe-soles was very interesting, and was the duty of every housewife. One saved up every scrap of old material or cuttings after preparing new garments. A large board table or a door taken off its hinges formed the basis for the work. All these tiny pieces are arranged on the board so that no two edges overlap, then the whole is covered with a layer of flour paste. This process is repeated until there are enough layers to give the required thickness. Then it is put in the sun to dry. The result is a kind of cardboard from which is cut the shape of a sole. Several layers of this are then sewn together with a cobbler-like stitch. A corresponding shape is then cut for the upper part of the shoe or boot which can be covered by nice silk, velvet, or cotton, hand embroidered, according to the type of footwear required. Such shoes only last about a month, so a mother with a big family will always be seen with a shoe-sole in her hand, as we of the West have our knitting to hand. All four of us wore such shoes after we had worn out our original supply of leather shoes.

Clanking Sword on the Stairs

After the surrender of Berlin, the Japanese ceased to be so friendly to us. One day when Mr. Koll was out on business, we heard the sound of a Japanese officer coming up the stairs, the dread sound of his long sword clanking as it hit each step, because the Japanese themselves are usually short in stature. He commanded the children and myself to sit down at the table after I had served the customary cup of tea.

He lectured the children through an interpreter on the evils of Communism saying they should always trust the Japanese. Then he challenged me, 'Why did the Germans give in?' When I expressed ignorance of the reason, he continued, 'They had all those soldiers in Berlin, why had they capitulated and why did I not know the reason?' I politely explained that in obedience to their commands we had no radio nor any other means of communication with the West, so we could not possibly know what was going on. Then he assured us that the Japanese would never give in but he was not sure as to what our position would now be under the new circumstances. He then demanded to make a plan of the house. Expressing my willingness, I produced pencil and paper for him, but it was soon obvious that he had no clue as to how to begin. When I offered to draw a plan for him, he accepted gladly. As he departed with the plan, he announced that it would be sent to headquarters and we would hear further.

Only a few days later the Chinese brethren came up to tell us that the 'Original Matter egg' had been dropped on Japan and that the war was over. After searching in the dictionary to find what this could mean and finding no answer as the dictionary was an old one, we realised it must be some modern weapon, for we had never heard of an atom bomb before. It soon became obvious that the rumour was true, for we heard no more of the officer and his plan, while the Japanese soldiers began to disappear from the city.

Chapter 19

The Communist Takeover

Although the end of the Sino-Japanese war had come, our hardest time had begun. As the Communists posed as helping Chiang Kai-Shek to liberate China from the Japanese, they were slowly getting the grip on China for themselves. For some time we had seen villages in the distance going up in flames. Daily the danger drew nearer to our city. We had already been selling hospital equipment and such things as the epidiascope, our cameras, etc., as we were needing the money and were quite aware that they would be confiscated if the city was taken. The pro-Japanese Mandarin had previously offered us gun-boat convoy if we wished to leave Hinghwa, but we did not wish to leave our dear Chinese friends to face the takeover alone. Moreover we had had no clear word from God to show that the Cloud had moved, although our children began to wonder if the Bible only contained 'waiting' texts.

At last in August, 1945, at the time of greatest heat, the sound of near gunfire in the middle of the night announced that the siege had begun. It had already been arranged that Ruth and Godfrey should go to the home of one of our Chinese Christian friends, as the defending army would probably want our hospital to use as a fort, since it was the only property in a good position higher than the city wall. I had already taken our woollen winter clothes from the attic where they were stored during the summer and put them into waterproof sacks and had them carried to the ground floor. When the whole of the back of the house was lit up by the bombs which were being thrown just outside the city wall, some of my students came and asked if they could take the sacks away to their more secluded homes. Shortly afterwards, the government ordered Mr. Koll and myself to evacuate the house, so I cut down the mosquito nets from the beds, packed up campbeds and sheets, while my husband made all other arrangements for the Chinese who lived in the house. Then we crept over the little bridge on the inland waterway at the double, since the latter was already under fire, and joined our children in the house of the Rong family.

How kind they were to take us in, for no one knew how the Communists would treat us foreigners, so it was at the risk of their own lives. The two children slept with their Chinese friends, while we both slept on the campbeds under the mosquito nets in the middle of the common visitors' hall. All the rooms of a better class Chinese house open on to an open courtyard with no access to the street so we could see nothing of what was taking place, only hear shells whizzing over the city and see the sky lit up by flames in the small square of it visible from the courtyard.

On the morning of the third day, the sound of firing ceased. The city had surrendered after a hard fight. Many Communists had lost their lives or been maimed, because they climbed up on to the city walls over the bodies of their fallen comrades, only to get their hands or fingers cut off by the defending troops, as they reached the top of the wall. As our hosts peered out of the main door, they could see the lines of grey-coated soldiers filing in, so we knew that we were conquered. A little later one of my students slipped in to advise my husband and myself to go home as our place was being looted. We bid our friends 'goodbye,' leaving arrangements for our children to be sent to Mlle. Junod in Nanking, should we not survive, then crept round the alleys near the city wall to get back home.

Looted!

What a sight greeted us! Soldiers were carrying out the things looted from the children's study, the dining-room clock was found lying at the bottom of the stairs, the empty boxes which had contained my wedding presents of silver, etc., not in daily use, were scattered in the garden or along the street.

At the main door, we were stopped by an officer and Mr. Koll was ordered upstairs. I was not allowed to go with him. Alone I waited, wondering whether I would hear a shot. But at last, after a thorough search, he was released and we were allowed to go into our flat on the top floor of the building. The study desk had been forced open with a bayonet, the curtains had been torn off the rails, the contents of my precious sewing box had been thrown into a pannier of flour which had been put to air in the sun as we always had to do in the hot, wet season. I use the word 'precious' because one cannot obtain tape, elastic and such-like haberdashery in the interior of China. In the bathroom, the bath-mat had been taken for a towel and on the floor were empty shell cases; under the goats' fodder in the outbuildings were rifles and pistols. In fact, everywhere was chaos, but by the grace of God we were able to restore some kind of order and were allowed by the Communists to live in our flat so that we could fetch the children back home.

For many days we could not even set a meal without an audience of soldiers. Soon the two lower storeys of the house were occupied by the 'Ministry of Health,' and the outlying buildings, formerly the isolation wards of the hospital, became the kitchen to feed about 150 troops. As they were all unaccustomed to the style of foreign houses, Mr. Koll was able to lock the door which connected the hospital floors with our flat and he also removed the handles so that no one would guess that there had been access. We then filled the whole staircase leading to the door with huge bundles of the straw which we used for firing our Chinese stove in the kitchen.

Interrogated!

From morning to night we were visited by the officers and other officials to interrogate us. We had to answer the same list of questions over and over again, where we were born, what we had done all our lives, why we were in Hinghwa, etc. As we looked out of our windows into the garden below, we could see our own property being used by the soldiery. Fish knives were being used with little effect, much to their dissatisfaction, for peeling fruit, while another would try to break up the steel belonging to the carving set since he did not know the proper use of it. In the meeting room, below our flat, they put the hospital patients; infectious diseases such as smallpox were all put together with surgical cases sleeping on the meeting-room benches. Drain pipes were stuffed with orange peel or cotton wool so that the waste water from our upper floor overflowed. Operations were performed and the amputated portion thrown out of the window. Instruments were sterilised in the same iron pans in which the morning meal had been cooked. Pigs were kept in the children's sandpit, mules stabled in the gate-house, and flocks of ducks were accommodated on the lawn, while the poor duck herder wept to our servants telling of how he had been pressed into service.

As all this took place at the height of the summer season, the stench was dreadful and yet we were kept from getting ill. After a kind of civil government was set up, my husband appealed that we might be freed from the constant visit of ordinary soldiers and so Wednesday and Sunday afternoons were fixed as our 'At Home' days. By midday, a queue of armed men led from our door halfway down the street. Mr. Koll would be in his study, I would stand in the dining room, Godfrey in the school room, Ruth in the bedroom and the Chinese amah in the kitchen as group after group were let in and given a conducted tour. This lasted for several hours each time, and each time the crowning astonishment was when they entered the bedrooms and discovered that the foreigners had a bed for each person. The longest delay was always in the school rooms, they stayed to squat in a circle to see Godfrey's fort and soldiers and other games which had not already been looted on victory day, for on the morning when we returned home, I had met one man carrying out his meccano set in the form of a battleship constructed a few days before the siege. To them, it would mean nothing more than a network of metal and screws which they might find useful.

Subversive Literature Discovered

Amid all the wearying interrogation, two outstanding crises of danger for us both occurred. The first happened a few days after the occupation. An officer came up into the dining room and accosted me with a Chinese songbook, demanding whether I recognised it. On my reply that I had never seen it before, he accused me of lying, saying that it had been found in the music rack of my school harmonium. When I still denied any knowledge of it, he turned to one page asking if I could read Chinese. Then he made me read one verse of a song, which spoke of the 'Red Bandits.' Then he ordered

me to go downstairs with him, at the same time refusing
to let Mr. Koll go with us.

I found a group of our young Chinese folk, including
Ruth and Godfrey, all sitting, white-faced round a
table. As he started to question me again, he turned the
book over so that I could read the name on the cover.
'Daniel Rong,' the English name chosen by one of our
teenage Christian boys. Again he urged all the young
people to speak the truth. Seeing how dangerous the
situation was getting, I edged a little nearer to Ruth and
whispered to her to tell her friend, who was Daniel's
sister, that she must own up. On that, she told him that
the book belonged to her brother.

At this point, I must explain that during the summer
holiday season, I had prepared two rooms in the ground
floor of the house, one for the boys and one for the girls,
where they could come and play games or sing with our
children, as there was no possibility of their going out
anywhere for recreation. Apparently the schoolbook
with which he had been supplied in the government
school had been used and left behind in the book rack of
the organ.

When the girl confessed, he sent for her mother, who
had been my faithful teacher and help from my earliest
days in China. She was a very tactful person and wise in
Chinese ways. 'Oh,' she said, 'How we have suffered
under the Japanese, seeing our children obliged to use
these pro-Japanese textbooks in the public schools. It
was careless of my boy to leave it here and surely Mrs.
Koll had never seen it.' Mollified by this patriotic
outburst and by her assurance that there was now no
longer need to use such books, he gave us all a warning
and departed, another answer to earnest prayer which
had been arising from all our hearts.

Brought before a People's Council

The other great danger arose about the woollen blankets

in the sacks which had been taken away by my students. One young Christian girl who lived near the North Gate, by which the Communists had entered the city, had my sack of best woollen blankets. Although she assured the soldiers that it belonged to the foreign missionary, even kow-towing to the ground beseeching them not to touch them, they each took a blanket and left her weeping. It was certainly a great loss since it is not possible to replace such things where we lived, but we were so glad to be alive and reunited with the children we did not worry much about it.

A few weeks later, however, an officer, with an escort, arrived to enquire about the blankets, saying that he had heard that we had lost them, but he wanted to assure us that the Communists never stole anything. After much tea-drinking and discussion on our part that we did not wish to have the blankets returned (one would not know who had used them anyhow and could not get them disinfected there), he insisted on having a detailed description of the goods. A few days later came a higher official and the same palaver took place. Then came one of still higher status. During the conversation with him, he asked if we had seen any of the blankets since the loss. Much against our will, we were obliged to give the information that our daughter had seen one of them in the possession of one of the soldiers billeted in the house of one of our friends. The next evening, about ten o'clock, we had a secret visit from one of my students whose father was in the Chamber of Commerce, warning us to refuse any further discussion on the blanket subject even if we were questioned again, because there had been a special council held, where the Red general had said, 'This devil Koll, whom we saved alive, has accused our soldiers of stealing.' So they had decided to hold a People's Council and bring Wilhelm up for investigation.

Now we know that such a trial is only a farce. A

representative from every family is forced to attend the public meeting. The accused is placed before them, the accusation is put forward, and then the question is shouted, 'to kill or not to kill' and death follows without further trial, either by being beaten to death or by shooting. If the crowd shout 'not kill,' then often another Council is held later consisting of people from another place where the prisoner is not so well known with the result that their desired end is attained. (This, of course, refers to that war period. Things are now different since there is a stable government.)

What could we do? There was only one way, to lay the whole matter before the Lord. This we did and waited. Shortly afterwards, the local garrison was sent to take another city to the north of us. At this battle, the Nationalists had sent bombers. These troops were not accustomed to air-raids and drew back, but our general rushed forward, urging them on, shouting that there was nothing to fear. Scarcely had he cried than a bomb fell and he was blown to pieces — a rather gruesome answer to our prayers — but we heard no more of the People's Council.

Difficult Living Followed

Then followed five months of very difficult living. Money grew scarcer as we could not obtain anything from the bank in Nanking, which was still in the hands of the Nationalists. We had our rice and wheat so there was no fear of starvation but we had to look round for things which we might sell to provide special needs. Mr. Koll had already helped some of our native labourers to set up small businesses of their own by giving them medicines and such like things from the old hospital dispensary. One worker set up a tiny general shop in the little riverside bookshop of the assembly at the East Gate. Some of the brethren who had a little capital had already formed a committee to organise a native soap factory, the profits of which were to be devoted to the Lord's work. As to ourselves, we had interesting adventures in selling some of our things. My dining-room clock, which had been my wedding present from the Chinese assembly, was exchanged for a load of straw to fire our Chinese oven for cooking.

One day I let the 'grapevine' carry the news to the former students that I was about to hold a sale of English books in our dining room. Among the articles were a great number of old annuals which the children did not want any more. To my great surprise, we sold out completely and the next day people were knocking at the door for more of the annuals. When I asked the amah why they were so popular, seeing that most folk could not read them in any case, she laughed and told me that such nice thick paper made excellent shoe-soles and everyone was eager to get more. Our cameras, epidiascope and much hospital equipment had gone long ago, so we were hard put to find anything more to sell.

Then our former cook, the dear fourth brother of the Chieh family, said, 'Give me the doll's house.' Now the doll's house was a very primitive affair according to toyland of our modern age, but when we returned to China in 1940, I had brought little gifts of furniture, etc., for future birthday presents, so it was well equipped with a three-piece suite, bedroom furniture, kitchen stove and proper bath and toilet with taps, while the dining room even had a canteen of cutlery. Off he went with the house and set it on the street before his dwelling. A few days later, back he came with a nice sum of money but he would not tell who had bought it. After the money was eaten in the form of pork and fish, he revealed that someone had decided that it would make a lovely home for his idol, but Lao IV (Chinese for 'fourth brother') would not tell me earlier lest I should have a conscience about using the money.

In spite of all the problems, we were glad to be able to remain in Hinghwa, for we were able to continue the assembly meetings by holding them in our flat. The rooms had been made to open into one another so as to allow the greatest current of air through during the very hot season, so we could seat quite a number of people by collecting every available chair, even the bathroom seat.

One Sunday morning is pictured very clearly in my mind. As we gathered round the Table to remember the Lord, the Communists, downstairs in the yard, were haranguing the people on the opium of religion that the Christians taught, while up above the clouds flew the Nationalist planes to machine-gun the city. For the first time I saw clearly what it meant, 'Thou preparest a table before me in the presence of my enemies.' One's heart could not but overflow in thankfulness that we had not fled away and left the Chinese Christians. All public school work, including the Sunday School, had to stop for we thought that it might be dangerous for the children, or at least offer a good chance for it to be taken over as an opportunity for propaganda. Many of the students tried to leave the city disguised as peasants.

One day an officer came to interrogate me about one of my students, who had been caught trying to get away. He did not mention any name so I was a little at a loss, because I had asked all of them never to tell me of their plans. At length, he mentioned the name of one of our Christian girls and demanded to know why she was going to be married to a soldier of the other army. 'Isn't she a Christian?' he said. I quite agreed that it was a pity but the engagement had been arranged by her heathen parents before she became a Christian. He replied, 'Why are her parents not also Christians?' Then I asked him politely if his honourable parents were still living, to which he answered that they were. 'Are they also Communists?' I asked. He replied in the negative. Then

I said, 'Why not, if you are a Communist?' This silenced him and this was often the best way to end an interrogation by letting them get caught in their own net.

As the months fled by and winter was drawing to a close, several things occurred which made us realize that it would be better to get our two teenage children away from the interior. Both of them were wise and aware of the traps which could be set but there was always the danger of the soldiers chatting in a friendly way with our children to get some handle against us. One day the officer of the songbook incident paid another visit. He was rather taken aback when he realised that I had recognised him. When I asked casually why they were so against Christianity if they believed in the three freedoms: speech, religion and press, he pointed his finger at my head, saying, 'You can think what you like there,' (then at my heart) 'You can feel what you like there! But if you were to say one word against us, we should not be as friendly as we have been hitherto.' Another time I was asked why I did not engage Ruth to a Communist. Also Godfrey was needing some dental attention; Mr. Koll had always done much dentistry for the family, including himself, and even for Japanese officers, but Godfrey had some teeth growing out of place as he had a small jaw, and my husband did not want to make a mistake by removing the wrong ones. Towards the end of January the Communists suddenly evacuated our house, giving us the chance to cleanse the hospital, especially the meeting room where a spade had to be used to scrape the floor before normal cleaning could begin. The hall was white washed and benches repaired so that we had the joy of seeing the assembly gathered together in its own place. We had already heard from Miss Willis in Shanghai that after she was released from internment at the end of the Japanese war, she was living in a camp run by the Canadian Relief

Committee, so that if the old house were set free we were welcome to use it, but at the moment it was still occupied by a Chinese general. Thus it seemed for us it was still 'wait.'

Chapter 20

Leaving Hinghwa*

At the time of the Chinese New Year in early February, there is always a national holiday with big feasting for five days, so there is no business and no post. On about the third day of the feast, two of our Chinese Christians came upstairs to tell us that there was a Christian boat-woman who would be willing to take us out if we wished. It was about 3 p.m. and we still had no indication that the Cloud had really lifted. The usual prayer meeting was held at 5 p.m. and the friends were just starting to go downstairs to it, saying that the boat could not wait if we did not feel free to go, when Ruth came bounding upstairs to say that there was a letter from Miss Willis brought by a private boat. On opening it we read, 'The house is free and the China Inland Mission is willing to take your two children into their boarding school temporarily.' This unexpected letter at a time when no post could usually arrive gave us the assurance that God's time had come to move.

Wilhelm went to the Red Civil Authority to get an exit pass, while we told the friends to accept the boat passage. I set to work to pack the most essential things;

---

*February, 1946.

other friends went to the corn merchants to negotiate the sale of our remnants of the last harvest so that we could have some ready money. It was of no use to take paper money as Communist notes were used in the city but were not negotiable over the next border. On route, pro-Japanese notes were still being used, but they, too, would be of no use in Shanghai where Nationalist money was used. So our dear Christian friend, Mr. Hung, obtained gold bars and rings for us. These I sewed into the collar of my husband's jacket and into the waist seams of his trousers. He would not allow me to carry any where the Chinese woman usually hid it, in the bun in her hair, for he did not wish me to be mauled about by the soldiers en route.

Twenty-four hours later, after a hasty farewell to all our dear Chinese friends, we loaded the boat up at dawn on the inland canal not far from the hospital. When God opens the door, no man can shut it.

Before we could leave the city, we had to pass through the water-gate, guarded by a watchman living in a straw hut at the side. There was still the question as to whether our luggage would be allowed to go through. But there had been a great victory won at some other town the previous day and the Reds had all been celebrating, so that there was no proper guard when the old man opened the gate and we passed through unchallenged.

Mr. Hsi and some other Chinese friends travelled with us, so we were tightly packed under the low roof shelter of the boat. We could sit or kneel but not stand up. Towards sunset we reached the border of 'No-Man's Land' but it was decided not to cross into the other territory until the next day. Mr. Hsi knew some peasants in a cottage nearby and suggested that we should sleep with them. We jumped ashore and, as Godfrey was feeling a little queasy after being so confined in a jerky boat, we walked round the back of the cottage. Presently Ruth joined us and said, 'Mummie, there is a man lying at the entrance to the cottage who has leprosy.' On investigation I found it was true and returned to the boat to discuss matters with the other friends. Finally it was decided that we four should remain in the boat for the night, while the others went quite happily to the cottage to occupy the bridal bed of the other son of the farmer who had been married a few days earlier.

Communist Territory Left Behind

An early start the next morning brought us quickly past the border guards without any difficulty and we were out of Communist territory. Soon we arrived at Taichow where we received a hearty welcome from the local Christians. We spent the next night with them. Meanwhile some gold was removed from Wilhelm's clothes and they hired a truck for the next stage of the journey. After an early breakfast, we issued forth at 6 a.m. to board the truck which was quite open with no roof or shelter, when to our dismay we found it was already packed tight with passengers. On our remonstrating that we had hired it for private use and had paid a very big price to have it to ourselves, the driver beamed upon us, saying that he was sure that we would not mind taking a few friends with us!

Chapter 21

Convert Becomes
the Keenest
of Christians

After crossing the Yangtse in a ferry boat, we reached the city of Chinkiang, where we met again our dear brother Ch'ang Kuo Chiang and his family, who had earlier managed to escape down river.

I must tell you about this young man. A few years earlier he had been training as a cinema operator in one of the units belonging to the Nationalist Government. The idea had been to prepare projection groups which would go to all the villages in the countryside to inform the people what the government was trying to do to improve the standard of living.

In the group, where Mr. Ch'ang was training, was a Christian officer, who talked to him about salvation through Jesus Christ. Although he was very interested, the time came for his final examination before he had made a decision. When he qualified, he was appointed to go with his apparatus to a new district, but before he departed this officer asked him again whether he would except Christ as his Saviour. When Mr. Ch'ang said that he did want to do so, they knelt in the snow and he yielded his life to his new Master. Then he expressed anxiety as to how he could learn more about the Bible. The officer told him to look out for a 'Jesus Hall' when he arrived in his appointed village, and to go and listen. If they preached that Jesus was the Son of God, that salvation was through the shed Blood and that the Bible was the inspired Word of God, then it was safe to join such a church.

Mr. Ch'ang landed in our out-station in the village of the White Foal (Poh Chu), where Gustav Koll had formerly worked. The assembly was now cared for by brother Hsi. After visiting the Gospel Hall, Mr. Ch'ang was convinced that here was the right place and he asked for baptism. Mr. Hsi hesitated at first, as it was usually done in fellowship with us in Hinghwa and usually took place at the East Gate baptistry during the New Year's conference, but Mr. Ch'ang was so urgent that they held the baptism in the local river and in this young convert we found one of the keenest practical Christians that we had amongst us.

Shortly afterwards the war reached our district and although he did his work faithfully for the Nationalist Government as long as he could, there came the day when he decided to bury his projector as a precaution against its falling into the hand of the enemy, and he himself was taken prisoner. His young wife was then left in a village near to Hinghwa and she was not a confessed believer, but she had heard from her husband that 'Whosoever called on the Name of the Lord would be saved,' without fully understanding what it meant. When the pro-Japanese army soldiers took over the village and came to rape her, as they did to all the young women, she shouted, 'I belong to the Lord Jesus, you cannot touch me.' She clung to the promise of the Name and God put His protecting arms around her and she was left unmolested.

All this I heard from her own lips later when she visited me, the first white woman she had ever seen. At first she came with fear and trembling, but later I became her 'mother' and her children were 'my grandchildren.' When her husband was released, they settled in Hinghwa and he obtained a small job. His first name had been, Kuo Ch'iang, meaning 'strong for my country,' but when he first became a Christian he changed it to 'Tsao Kuang' which means, *Seeking the Light* and later again to 'Fah Kuang,' *Shining out the Light* (As there was no proper registration of names, one could change at will). In his life, he carried out literally the changes he had made to his name.

Taking the Lord's Words Literally

One could give many illustrations of how literally brother Ch'ang took the Lord's words but one stands out in my mind. One day he brought his little girl with a very bad eye infection. We took her into the hospital and my husband treated her every day until she was better. Then as we handed her over to her father, I said, 'Now be very careful of infection. Have you any other case in the courtyard where you have rooms?' 'Oh yes, the family who live opposite all have bad eyes.' So I added the warning never to lend towels or such things. 'But I cannot help that,' he answered, 'The Lord Jesus said that if you have two coats, you must give to him that has none. Now they have no towel, so I lend them mine.' What can one answer to such a person? I did the only possible thing and gave him extra towels.

This was the tone of his life. If anyone in the assembly had a problem, he would sit up all night to do some repairs. Then came the time when he was seized by the Communists as one who had helped the Nationalist Government, but in answer to prayer the whole family managed to escape down river and that is why we had the joy of meeting them again.

With a beaming face he met us at the ferry and led us to his 'home,' full of praise to the Lord for having made provision for them. It was taken for granted that we should share their meal. We were led to a tiny little shoe shop, whose owner had let them a tiny room in the roof to sleep and a little platform overlooking the shop where they could eat.

There we enjoyed much fellowship with boxes as seats around a table, the only piece of furniture they seemed to possess. In the attic room they just spread their bedding rolls on the floor, but there was not the slightest hint of complaint either from him or his wife, only shining faces telling how God had preserved them. He was earning just enough to provide the daily rice by making small electric torches and charging the batteries on a plug in the shop. While the men-folk were talking, I had a quiet chat with Mrs. Ch'ang and she told me that they shared even to their last bowl of rice with every new party of refugees which came down river but she assured me that the heavenly Father always sent some more. How greatly I would like to see where they are now.

Farewell to the Kolls, December 15, 1946, with Miss Helen Willis
(second row, second left) and Chinese Christians

Chapter 22

To Shanghai in Safety

From Chinkiang we boarded the train for Shanghai, where we arrived towards evening. At the station we hired an open truck, loaded our boxes and with them set off for the compound of the Willis' family. The garden we found lying under several inches of water due to recent floods, so wading along planks, we arrived at the caretaker's room. There, to our dismay, we were told that the upstairs was occupied. The lower storey was rotten with damp, so that my amah found her leg going through the floor. (She was the mother of 'Precious Fragrance' who had insisted on going with us to help in Shanghai.) We just didn't know what to do. The letter had said that the house was free and that the children would be accommodated. They had been so often assured during all the trials that all would be better when we reached Shanghai.

It was nearly sunset so we decided that Mr. Koll should go out and buy some bread, butter, (which we had not seen for many years) and tea, while we waited to see what we could do for the night. Then suddenly the door burst open and there stood the daughter of my old friend Mrs. Ruck, Frieda Foggin, and her husband George, loaded with shopping goods.

After much hugging and explaining, we found that the formidable people occupying upstairs were not Chinese generals or soldiers but only our dear friends the Foggins and their children with one other missionary lady, who had been left in charge while the parents went shopping and who, on hearing us all talking Chinese when we arrived, thought that it was a new Chinese invasion and had hastily locked the door. How we laughed, while Frieda led us upstairs and George insisted that we eat the meal which they had prepared for themselves.

The Foggin family had been forced to evacuate from right over on the borders of Tibet, travelling mostly in cattle trucks, so they knew how we felt. They expected to be only a few days in Shanghai so we all decided to do the best we could together. It was too dark now to see about beds, so Wilhelm and I swept away a little of the dust from the floor of another unoccupied room, spread our oiled sheeting covers from the bedding-bundles, opened the bed-rolls and settled the children to sleep on the floor, while we chatted to the Foggins for a time. They had three children with them and were expecting the arrival of another quite soon, which was the reason they were trying to get air-transport to Peking to her parents as soon as they could. This was possible for them as they were Canadians and could get help from their government. Finally with the aid of one electric torch, we also crept into our bed on the floor and peace pervaded the house of refugees until we awoke to a new chapter in our lives, seven months refugeeing.

Shanghai, Friends and Visitors

After a few days the Foggins got a flight in a 'United States' plane to Peking and we took possession of the room and the verandah room where they had been living. The little verandah room with windows on all sides had been turned into a bathroom by the Willis family when they were in residence, but we placed a bamboo frame over the bath and made a bed for my husband, while I slept in the bed in the L-shaped room when it had been de-bugged and disinfected after the army occupation. The little verandah room also served as dining room and lounge when Mr. Koll's bed was rolled up in the morning. Our two children went for a time as boarders to the China Inland Mission's Home for the children of their own German-speaking missionaries, while they attended some classes left over from the closed German school. Soon, even these classes closed, one after the other as the German teachers were gradually repatriated. Godfrey was the first to come home. Then he went to the British Government School. He slept on a camp bed in the long arm of the L-shaped room. Our dining room cum lounge cum bedroom was very pleasant and many a happy meal we shared there with young Christians from the U. S. forces or the British Navy.

On Sunday we found a corner downstairs where we could put a table and chairs so that we could entertain our Chinese friends, who came down, one group after another, to refugee in the port city of Shanghai. Upstairs I obtained a one-ring electric plate, but the Chinese food was mostly cooked on charcoal stoves out-of-doors by our little Chinese amah, who thoroughly enjoyed being hospitable. She never decided until after the meeting how much to cook, because we did not know how many guests we should have. By this time Mr. Koll had mended the leaking roof of the verandah and patched some of the rotten floors on the ground-floor with pieces of petroleum tins.

Later, dear Miss Willis also came to join us, living at the other end of the verandah, after she left the Canadian camp for internees who had been released from the Japanese concentration camps. During the war

and the Japanese occupation of Shanghai, many of the
out-reach activities of their meeting in Shanghai had
been stopped. Just behind the house where we were
living was a large encampment of straw huts housing
the many Chinese refugees from up country, so we felt
that something should be done about a Sunday School
for the swarms of children, although we did not know
whether they would understand our dialect. However,
we opened the doors on Sunday afternoon and the
crowd poured in, children mostly barefooted and some
in their birthday dress only. Mr. Koll guarded the door
while I started a chorus. What would happen? A great
shout arose, "She speaks our 'North of the River'
dialect." It turned out that most of these people came
from our Grand Canal area, so the school thrived and
was continued by Miss Willis and her helpers long after
we left.

One brother, who helped her there and in the now re-
established Bible bookshop, was the fifth brother of the
Chieh family of the 'White Foal' village, Poh Chu, our
out-station, so he also spoke the North River language.
Later this dear man was imprisoned for preaching the
Gospel in the open air and finally died in a labour camp
in the mines.

We also had many other visitors from our own
Hinghwa who had also escaped from the Communists.
Our dear Mr. Hung, who had always been such a friend
was one of these, but he was very ill with cancer and
died soon afterward on the operating table in a Nanking
hospital. It was also the good hand of God upon him
because he was one of the rich land-owners of Hinghwa
and although he had been such a good landlord that
none of his farmers would denounce him, the
Communists would surely have executed him at some
time on some trumped-up excuse.

Dear Mr. and Mrs. Hsi also paid us a visit telling us of
God's wonderful deliverance for them. Quite early,

while we were still in Hinghwa, their son, Samuel (who had been born in answer to prayer, hence his name) had escaped from the city. They had received some letters from him and had hidden them under one corner of the bed-frame. Not long afterwards the Communist soldiers came to interrogate them turning the whole place upside down in the process, even digging a hole in the floor to see if letters were hidden. With tears in her eyes, Mrs. Hsi told me how they stood and prayed that the letters would not be found. Then came the awful moment when they started searching the bed, but they lifted every corner except the one where the letters were hidden. So God puts His hand over His children.

Leaving Shanghai Without Mr. Koll

Meanwhile we were trying to get a visa to re-enter Britain. Day after day we joined the crowd at the British Embassy but we still had our German passports. At last permission was given for the children and myself, because I was British-born but a visa for my husband was definitely refused and no hope was given for the future. We had been nine months in Shanghai already, so we finally decided that I should first return with the two children. Ruth was 16 and Godfrey 14 years old and it was time to find a way for them to earn their living. After some further waiting, we obtained passage on an English troop-ship in December, 1946. Never shall I forget the moment when I stood at the stern of the vessel and saw Wilhelm turn away to go back alone to the Shanghai house.

We spent Christmas with the Colliers in Hong Kong and reached England on January 26th, 1947. Owing to the war conditions, my sister had been obliged to let part of our bungalow in Iver Heath, so we could not go home but a very kind friend, Mr. Whear, in Ickenham, opened up his home to us and we were able to settle into the upstairs flat. It was wonderful to be able to see

Mother once more but it was only for a very short time, because the Lord called her Home at the age of 84 years only three weeks after our arrival. This led the young couple who were sharing the home at Iver Heath to decide to move out to make room for us, so that by May-June we were able to move in and prepare a place in case Wilhelm should be able to return to us from China.

At Easter we three were invited to go to Hull in Yorkshire for the Conference. Just the day before our departure we received a letter from China, saying that my husband had no hope of getting permission to come to England. On that same evening I wrote a letter to the Secretary of State putting my case before him. When the brothers at Hull heard the position, it was decided to hold a special prayer-meeting on the Saturday afternoon on Mr. Koll's behalf. Many were present and the prayers were earnestly devoted to the subject in hand. One prayer was 'Lord, please break the red-tape.' After the conference, the children and I went to relations in Wiltshire for a short stay. On the Saturday following the Hull Conference, I was sitting in a deck-chair on the lawn, when my cousin came running with a cable from China in her hand. When we tore it open, we read, 'Visa granted, Wihelm.' What a flood of joy fills the heart at such wonderful answers to prayer. I received no written reply to my letter to the Home Office but they must have communicated at once with Shanghai to grant the permit.

Chapter 23

Re-Entering English Life

Once the children and I were settled in our Iver Heath home which we shared with my then unmarried sister, there began the problem of their further education. Ruth decided at once to follow a correspondence course to enable her to pass the English matriculation examination. Godfrey accompanied me to a Junior Technical College for an interview but we were told that they could not give a place to a German boy in preference to an English boy. Thus he too started a correspondence course which we could follow at home.

Meanwhile the next important step was to get them naturalised as British subjects as soon as possible. During the war, the law concerning British women married to aliens had been altered. When I was caught in England at the outbreak of war in 1939, I applied to see if I could get back my British citizenship, but I was informed that this could only be done if my husband were deceased. In 1947, however, I was able to apply for renaturalisation and on the forms I asked that the two children, both minors, might be included. Mine was immediately granted, but for the children it was refused. The next step was to apply for them separately but this would mean the payment of £ 20 which we did not have at that moment, so we went to prayer and, after a short time, received what we needed for the application to be sent in.

Meanwhile we applied to the Education Department at Senate House to see if it were possible for Ruth to receive a four-year teacher training course with academic study such as I myself had done. When the appointment arrived I saw at the head of the form the name of the director, which seemed to fit in with the initials of my former professor of Applied Mathematics and Mechanics, who had gone to prison as a pacifist during the First World War. After Ruth and I had talked with the secretary, I ventured to ask if this gentleman mentioned as the director of Senate House belonged to the Society of Friends. On her reply in the affirmative, I asked if I might speak to him, but she said it would be quite impossible as he was interviewing all the candidates for the next four-year course.

As we rose to leave the office, I sent up my wireless message to the One who had never failed me and before we closed the door, who should walk in but the gentleman himself. At once we recognised each other and he asked me why I was there, since he knew that I had gone to China. When I explained the situation he told me not to worry at all, he could assure me that Ruth could have her training free. Was that not another case of 'bread cast upon the water which would return after many days?' Later that week I received a letter from him guaranteeing a full four-year course of training if I could get Ruth naturalised.

Naturalising the Children

One afternoon as I returned from speaking at a meeting, the children told me that a policeman had called, leaving the message that I was to ring up a certain number in Whitehall. When I did so, an appointment was made for me to have an interview. On arrival I was ushered into the presence of a very kind gentleman, who explained that he wished to make certain enquiries concerning my application for naturalisation of the children. Apparently the authorities hesitate about doing this for minors because, in some cases, the children later wish they had retained the nationality of the father. So he asked me for what special purpose I needed it for my daughter. In my pocket I had the letter from the Director of Senate House and when I produced it for him to read, he expressed complete satisfaction about Ruth.

Then he referred to Godfrey. When I told him he had been refused a place at the Junior Technical College because of his nationality, and that he was so sure he wanted to become British he was already planting trees in the garden which he could enjoy at a later date, this clinched the matter for him too. During the course of conversation I had been asked a little about our circumstances as to house and finance, so there was opportunity to witness to the triumph of a life of faith in God alone.

After the gentleman was satisfied as to the reasons for naturalisation, he said diffidently that there was another question which arose which he had considered too delicate to discuss on the telephone. How did I stand as regards the extra £ 20 needed for the papers. (If the children had been included in my papers it would have cost only five shillings.) Then I told him how we three had prayed God for the money and we now had it in hand. 'But' I said, 'if there is any other way by which we need not pay the full sum, I should be glad, because we could use the money for God in another way!' 'Well,' he replied, 'there is, but after my conversation with you this morning I wonder whether you will use it. You must fill in a form saying you are abjectly poor with no resources.' My reply was simple: 'Oh, no, I have trusted my heavenly Father to supply all my need for over thirty years and I would not so dishonour His Name as to say that I was in such a condition.' 'Then there is no other way but to pay,' was his reply.

We parted glad to have had the opportunity to discuss the matter and I left the whole thing in the hands of God. Shortly afterwards I received a letter from Whitehall telling me to send back my own naturalisation papers and they would include the names of the two children in them, so I never had to pay the £ 20.

Chapter 24

Reunited as a Family

In July, 1947, Godfrey and I were able to go up to Liverpool to meet Wilhelm who had managed to get a passage on a troop-ship just as we had done; ours had landed in Southampton. Mr. and Mrs. Bunt welcomed us to their home at Prescot to await his arrival. What a joy it was to be re-united and soon we were settled back in Iver Heath as a happy family. There was a big garden and orchard so we were kept busy, not only growing our own vegetables but bottling fruit and storing apples. The soil was very good and had little chalk, so Godfrey not only had the joy of planting trees and making a pond, but also growing rhododendrons and azaleas and it was like a little paradise apart from the weeds, which had to be eradicated all the time, especially as we were often away frim home visiting the different assemblies in England.

Ruth passed her matriculation examination in September, 1947, but she was just too young by a few days to enter college that year, so she filled in the time in a local school as a student teacher, which stood her in good stead when she finally entered for teacher training the following year.

To Switzerland for Meetings

In 1951, my husband and I were invited to visit the meetings in Switzerland and this led to a new peep at the Golden Thread. Our bank balance was very low at that time and we had to provide for the running of the household in our absence. When this was done we were faced with the question as to whether we could pay our fares to the Continent and leave only a few shillings in the bank. There was such a thing as rates and taxes connected with the house and land. However, we set off by boat and train for Zurich, where we started the visits because our German was better than our French, so that in Lausanne we would need an interpreter. After many journeys in German Switzerland, we proceeded to Lausanne.

One afternoon, Mr. Jean André, who has three children's holiday homes in the Jura Mountains, took us by car to visit Jura Rosaly, which was then occupied by a group of German children. This big work started just after the Second World War, when Mr. André was in Germany on business and saw on the station in Frankfurt the crowds of refugee families. Within two months he had large convoys of about 70-80 German children having good food, loving care, and above all hearing the story of the love of God and His way of salvation through the death of His beloved Son.

At first these groups stayed for periods of three months until they were restored to normal health. That afternoon visit was my first introduction to this work which was to alter the course of my life for many years to come. On one of the days of our stay in Lausanne, I was asked to speak to the ladies while Mme. Jean André translated for me. After the meeting she said to me, 'Would you be willing to come and help us in the German camps? My husband gets so little time at home because of the continual camp work as well as his own business commitments.' (The André brothers have business interests all over the world.) At first I gave a very vague promise to see what I could do, but God was leading me into a new work, which would fill the emptiness which seemed to come when we found that we would probably never be able to return to China after the Communists took over the whole country.

German Swiss Camp Helper

The following year the fulfilment of my promise was claimed, although I protested that my German was not so good as that of a German speaker; I was plunged in and helped with the Bible courses in two German camps.

In the next year, 1953, this developed into the venture of taking English children for periods of ten weeks. It was the time of the big floods on the East Coast of England and Mr. André invited us to bring a group of those who had lost their homes in the spring and another group in the autumn, all at his expense. So I became the collaboratorof Mr. Charles Clark of Brentford who had formerly taken groups from his own district for shorter periods.

These first two camps were for periods of five weeks and the flood victims were gathered by the International Help for Children. Just before the spring camp was due to start, we received a telegram to say that it could not be held in Jura Rosaly owing to shortage of water, so we were to travel to Chateau d' Oex in the Alps, where we were to occupy two chalets. Mr. Sewell, our missionary in Guyana, was in Switzerland at the time taking a heart cure, but as his cardiogram had just reached a satisfactory stage, he came to help with the spiritual work. We had a wonderful time and young souls came to know the Lord Jesus as their own personal Saviour. Since then grandchildren of these early campers have been to our Swiss camps and a relation of one of them, also a camper, has been helping in the Operation

Mobilisation in France. The autumn camp was held in Jura Rosaly as was planned.

Camp Children from England Increase

The following year Mr. Clark and I started selecting the children ourselves and the whole work was organised under the name of the Brentford Town Mission, because one must have some kind of a name in order to get the necessary collective passport. The responsibility before the Home Office was taken by Mr. Clark, but if I remember rightly he at first had a problem when the official wanted to interview the real head of the organisation and he was able to say that would not be possible as He was in Heaven.

At first we took children from all parts of England, which involved approaching the education authorities of each separate county to get the permits for the children to be absent from school for such long periods. At the same time we had to guarantee to have a qualified teacher in the camp and to give a certain fixed number of hours of instruction each day. Most of the campers came from poor homes, or homes where there was overcrowding or some other domestic problem. Later the work became concentrated in the Brent area where we had an education officer who was very sympathetic to the work. It would take up too much space in this book to give details of all the sixteen camps where I had the privilege of serving, but the work still goes on.

I was obliged slowly to resign the reins as my dear husband became older and unable to look after himself completely, as he had graciously done during my long absences. During the early camps he had often been away himself, visiting the meetings, but later when he felt too old to do those long itineraries, he cared for himself, cooking, cleaning and gardening, doing, as he always said, his share. From the beginning our married

life had always entailed such a fifty-fifty sharing of all
the work, so that the main purpose of our life could take
its course at all costs.

Miss Ann Dakin, who had worked with me in the
camps, was the first to take over complete responsibility,
and after several years of faithful service she left to train
for missionary work abroad. At the time of writing, she
has already done a year's work in Java and hopes to
establish an orphanage there for Javanese children.
Several of our former helpers are now telling others
about 'our great salvation' in lands abroad, Vietnam,
Kenya, Zambia, the Philippines and South Africa. The
number of children, who go to Switzerland each year,
now has doubled as Mr. André has been able to allocate
two of his houses to the English children. We now have
a house in the Brent area where some workers live, who
are able to follow up the children on their return home
by holding regular Bible clubs in the district, or visiting
their homes.

Jobs, Marriages and Grandchildren

Meanwhile our two children had both trained and
started their own jobs, one as a teacher and the other as
a municipal engineer. Now both are happily married
with partners who love the same Lord and employ their
spare time in serving Him. There are also six grandchildren ranging (in 1972) from four to seventeen years
of age, and to our joy the older ones are already
witnessing for the Lord. One can only look back and
marvel when one thinks of the long evenings when
Wilhelm and I walked backwards and forwards in our
flat on moonlit evenings in China wondering what
might happen to our children, shut in as we were with
no artificial light by which we could read and no
apparent opportunity for preparing them for taking
their place in a modern world. Yet we always fell back
on the promise, 'to thee and thy seed after thee.'

About four years ago, another of our earnest prayers was answered in a special way. My sister, who shared the property in Buckingham-Shire with me, had already married but owing to the fact that I had no fixed salary or income, it did not seem possible for me to arrange to pay out her share of the inheritance; and although she always declared that she was not in need of the money, the debt lay on my heart. Then suddenly, without our seeking it, someone from an estate agent called one Monday evening asking if I were willing to sell the property as they wanted it, with some other houses, for development.

The whole business took some time to be brought to a conclusion but in the end, I was able to give my sister the share which was more valuable than if I had been able to pay her when she married and, moreover, was able to buy a small bungalow in Eastbourne where my husband and I could live. How often answers to our prayers are delayed so that the Lord can do exceedingly above all that we ask or think.

In September, 1969, we moved to Eastbourne where we were welcomed so lovingly by the assembly there. My dear husband could only enjoy the new home for a year, after which he had an operation for cataract, successful in itself, but one from which he never recovered physical strength. He seemed to break down and, for the following year, he was a complete invalid, but we were able to nurse him at home. It was a very difficult time, one in which one learned what the love and fellowship of other dear Christians really means. At any hour of the day or night, I was able to telephone and someone would come to help.

In the autumn of 1971, the Lord took him to be with Himself, something for which he had yearned for a long time for he had nearly reached the age of ninety. For some months I had to go very slowly after an attack of angina pectoris which had come as the result of the

Outside Bourne Hall, Eastbourne, Sussex, England, circa 1969/70.
Mrs. Koll (extreme left) and Mr. Koll (on her left)

In the house of Mr. Hans Gschwind and his sisters at Zurich,
Switzerland. Left to right: Miss B. Gschwind, Mrs. Weston, Mr. Weston,
Mr. H. Gschwind, Mrs. Koll and Mr. Koll and Miss M. Gschwind.

heavy lifting entailed in the long nursing period, but by the good hand of our God there was a good recovery.

Chapter 25

Air Ticket to Hong Kong *

Then just about Christmas time came a great shake-up when a letter arrived from German Switzerland containing a gift of money, 'labelled' 'towards your journey to Hong Kong.' It had always been a wish in my heart to go back as near as I could to the land where most of my life had been spent, but the question was as to whether my health and age would now stand up to it there.

After much prayer, I took the first step by going to see my doctor, asking for a complete check-up so that I could know whether I could fly. He raised his eyebrows and asked 'Fly where?' 'Oh, only to Hong Kong,' I replied. He smiled and proceeded with the examination with the result that he pronounced the blood pressure back almost to normal and, as far as he could see, there was nothing to hinder the trip.

From then on things began to move. I made enquiries as to route and costs. The sea trip would have been my choice, but I found that since the Suez Canal was closed, one must make a long and expensive journey via Cape Town and then Darwin in Australia and from there a ship for Hong Kong.

---

* *1972.*

From my dear friend, Miss Helen Willis, came a great welcome to Hong Kong though she had to confess with regret that she could not put me up in her home because they had several refugees who had swum across from Red China, so that all her rooms were occupied. Two of these were the sons, about 16-17 years of age, of one of their adopted Chinese girls, who was married in Canton province. Helen suggested, however, one or two alternatives for accommodation. Meanwhile I approached our brethren in England to see how they felt about my going, and I received encouragement from all sides. My first thought was to take a return ticket to Hong Kong and from there visit Taiwan, so that I planned to leave England in April, but just then came a suggestion that I should visit the Missionary Conference in Jamaica scheduled for the beginning of May. This meant my putting my trip to an earlier start in the middle of March. Through the Crusade Travel Organisation, enquiries were made to get cheaper flights but my good friends in England said there were too many changes that way and insisted that I travel ordinary passenger fare.

The Lord Said 'Come'

Before I had started on any real moves, I prayed the Lord that He would give me a Word to stand on as He had always done in all my important decisions. It came from the well-known story of the storm on the lake, not so much from the final stilling of the waves, but that the Lord, knowing Peter's heart, said to him, 'Come.' I felt the Lord was saying this to me, so like Peter, I began to walk, but one can always expect the big waves. Several rollers had already been overcome, the doctor's permit, the completion of all the injections for cholera, typhoid, and vaccination, the giving of Helen's welcome, the generosity of friends all over Europe.

Then I began to make enquiries as to obtaining a visa for Taiwan. The central telephone exchange could only give me one possible connection, but the only reply came from a dictaphone. 'We do not issue tourist visas for Taiwan.' Here was a setback but the Lord whispered 'Look at Me, not at the wind and the waves.' As I calmed down, I remembered that we knew of someone who had returned as a missionary to Taiwan only a few weeks previously. I telephoned the headquarters of the O.M.F. and they gave me a telephone appointment with the Transport Officer for that afternoon. So I first went quietly to have my siesta and then got in touch with him. The problem seems to have arisen since Taiwan was put out of the U.N, whereupon the consulate in Brussels closed. The only way left was to contact Madrid which would take a long time. So he told me how their missionaries obtained a visa and advised me to wait until I reached Hong Kong. Thus a new big wave receded.

The next arose when the time drew near for my departure and as yet my completed ticket had not arrived. I telephoned to say that I was leaving Eastbourne so they agreed to bring it to the airport, as I was spending the weekend with my daughter in Pinner. On Monday, March 13, my son-in-law, Len Reveley, and Ruth drove me to Heathrow. There Mr. Clark was also waiting to see me off, so we stood waiting and chatting, but no ticket. Secretly I raised my heart to the One who had bid me 'Come' and slowly the clock ticked on until nearly the time when I must register the luggage. Then just in time the lady from the travel bureau ran up, explained the delay and gave me the completed ticket, upon which there followed a quick farewell and the long journey had started.

Chapter 26

Sixteen
Floors Above
Hong Kong

The trip itself was wonderful. During the afternoon we came down at Frankfurt in Germany, while our next stop was at Beirut at 10 p.m. where one could see nothing but streaming torrential rain. About 2 a.m., we landed at Tehran in Iran and as there was no further stop registered until we were due in Bangkok, I decided to close my eyes for a little sleep. It seemed to be only a short time later that I drew the shutter of the side window expecting still only to find darkness, but I had forgotten that with each mile of flight eastwards, we were putting the clock forwards.

What a sight greeted my eyes! Dawn over the Himalayas, the snow-capped peaks all rosy with the morning light and below us the long serpentine coils of the river Ganges wending its way across the great northern plain of India. This decided me against any further naps. Presently another great river flowed down from due north and joined the Ganges — probably the Brahmaputra, and soon we were over the delta country of Burmah, riddled with rivers and canals embracing the green paddy fields, until we crossed over Rangoon, to fly on to Thailand. When we came down in Bangkok, there was an influx of passengers, mostly Thai or

Chinese, on their way to Hong Kong with a sprinkling of Europeans who were travelling beyond that to Sydney in Australia. The last stretch of the journey lay over Cambodia, Laos and Vietnam, but then directly over the South China Sea up the coast of China until we landed at the airport in Kowloon where dear Helen Willis awaited me.

Met by Helen Willis

We soon sped by taxi to the big, newly opened YWCA in Man Fuk Road where she had booked a room for me, but my heart sank as a new wave reared its head when the receptionist said, 'Yes, floor 16!' Now I had always had a real phobia about automatic lifts when they had no attendant because I had been shut in one on a previous visit to Germany and did not know how to get out.

During the following four weeks, new grace helped me to overcome this completely because I had to go up and down alone so many times a day that it became normal procedure. It was a very comfortable room with a writing desk, a nice bed, an armchair and a private shower room and toilet. The first thing that greeted me was a Gideon Bible in Chinese and English on the writing table. From the window I would look out on to the neighbouring block of flats, like ours, twenty storeys high, and away up the street, crowded with cars looking like ants crawling along, to the hill whose top was to be sheared off and its sides cut into deep terraces so that a new block of flats could be erected to house the refugee population from Red China just over the border.

Hong Kong itself is an island, and contains most of the British government buildings, while in its centre rises the mountain called the 'Peak.' To reach the Island from Kowloon where I was staying and where Helen Willis lived and worked, we had to use the ferry steamer. Kowloon is on the mainland and was leased to Britain in 1899 for a hundred years. In addition to this fairly great stretch of land, which contains the airport, thickly populated and covered with skyscrapers, is an area which was rented from the Chinese at a later date and on not so firm a lease called the New Territories, which goes right out to the border with Red China separated from it by a big river. This is the one over which the refugees try to swim. Hundreds try to cross every week seeking freedom in a free country. Many are captured or shot before they reach the river, others are drowned on the way, but thousands have reached Kowloon and whole hillsides are covered with rudely constructed huts, made of bits of tin, wood, cardboard, forming the shanty towns, where the refugees live until the British government of Hong Kong can build enough flats to house them.

These newest buildings consist of about twenty storeys; on each floor are two large living rooms separated by a kind of bridge corridor in which are the communal kitchen and bathroom. A family must consist of at least four members to have a right to occupy one of these living rooms and it often happens that there are many more than four but it is a paradise compared with the shanty town where they were living before. Three such blocks form what is called a village community. Some of the older blocks, slightly lower than the newest flats, perhaps twelve or fourteen storeys, have on the roof accommodation for a primary school.

Roof-Top School

Many of the mission societies have taken the opportunity of forming and running such a school. One of these is run by Mr. Collier, the brother-in-law of Miss Willis. There on the roof is a lovely school of 250 children, mostly drawn from the flats below. Daily these children are taught of the love of God and His Word. Brother Collier is over 80 years of age, has had a stroke so that he is lame and must walk with two sticks, yet he mounts these stairs twice daily to care for his school. (There are no lifts in these old buildings.) Miss Willis feared for me to try to get up there, but I cannot resist a school, so I took a heart pill at the bottom, not daring to look up to see how many stairs there were to climb and finally spent a happy morning with the dear children on the roof.

Christian Book Room, Kowloon

Although Helen Willis begins to look old and worn, she does a full day's work right round the year. Twice a day she travels from the foot of the hills, where they have a house next door to the school building of Miss Majorie Hayhoe, across the dusty hot traffic-jammed streets of Kowloon to her Christian Book Room* which is a mail order depot and not a sales shop with an opening direct on to the street. Bible texts in many languages, translations of many of the books of older brethren with many of their own publications are mailed all over the world, especially where there are large Chinese populations.

One of her regular tasks is the preparation of the Chinese-English Calendar issued each year. On each leaf is the text-for-the-day printed in Chinese and English (I use one everyday, covering up the English at first to make sure that I can still read the Chinese so as to keep up my knowledge of the language). Apart from the day's work in the bookshop, Helen keeps house for the rest of their missionary group, Mr. Collier, Miss Hayhoe, Mr. Pilkington and the Chinese refugee lads.

---

*Christian Book Room, 108 Boundary St., G/F., Kowloon, Hong Kong. P.O. Box 95413, Tsim Sha Tsui, Kowloon, Hong Kong.

500-Pupil School

Next to the house where they live is the big school of
over 500 Chinese children which is still run by Miss
Hayhoe, who is also over 70 and is suffering from an
incurable nerve disease. There are morning and
afternoon sessions each of 250 children. Both schools
are recognised by the government and pupils can sit for
the state examinations, but as they are not registered,
they are not subsidised so that they have perfect liberty
to teach the Bible.

The playground round the house is full of children all
day long even after school hours, when the children of
the whole neighbourhood are free to come and play, a
great boon as you would realise if you could see the
narrow lane bordered by one-storey shops through
which one must pass to reach their compound. Such
shops form also the living and sleeping quarters for the
family of the owners.

I felt at home in all this noise and activity and only
wished I were 30 years younger and could begin all over
again. In this happy household with its few amenities,
there was never a complaint about their age or
infirmities, only joy in service and not one seemed to
wish to retire to their home country. 'Work while it is
day,' appeared to be the motto.

Message Sent to China

One of the chief purposes of my visit to the Far East was
to see if I could send a message to some of our former
Christian friends on the mainland. To my joy I found it
was possible on a rare occasion, so off it went using
only the Chinese Christian names of my two children.
So far there has been no reply but I do pray that they
may have been gladdened by the knowledge that we
care and pray for them.

Bible 'House Churches' and Mission Work

The greatest uplift of all was to find that Bibles were now getting into Red China again. At a big interdenominational prayer meeting held in one of the large hotels in Kowloon, we were able to hear the leader of this work tell thrilling stories of how God is blessing this service; of the large number of Bibles which are getting into China, of the large number of real believers that are still all over that huge country, of how they encourage one another by meeting in little groups of two or three.

There is no smuggling of the Bibles, they are carried in openly. The New Testament is now printed in Hong Kong in the new phonetic script taught in all schools on the mainland. Now, contrary to the olden days, compulsory education is enforced for all children. Moreover, later news since my return, shows that more liberty is being granted for small groups to gather and still more Bibles are being allowed to go in. How truly is it again being proved, as it was at the time of the Boxer persecution, that the blood of the martyrs is the seed of the Church.

During my four weeks in Hong Kong, friends took me to visit many other kinds of work being done for the Lord. One day we took a trip right out into the New Territories to see the 'House of Loving Kindness,' a beautiful building in lovely surroundings, where some young Christian ladies devote their lives to caring for spastic Chinese children. They had to leave their original premises but managed to get this mansion, however, they can only develop one room at a time as the Lord sends gifts to meet the expenses. On the way we went out to the Border between British and Communist territory and my heart felt very homesick as I viewed the land where much of my life had been spent.

Soon after my arrival in Kowloon, Miss Willis and I took the ferry across to the main island, where I managed to get my visa for Taiwan. We also went up in the Peak tram to the top of the mountain from which one gets a magnificent view of the whole harbour. The last time I had been there was in 1946 when the children and I had spent a day in Hong Kong on the way home to England. Then it was desolate, for everywhere were the ruined buildings left after the recapture from the hands of the Japanese. Now the coastline is marked by modern skyscrapers. Hong Kong is a wealthy city.

At Elsie Koll's home at Eastbourne with George and Frieda Foggin
(of Taiwan) and daughter Joy

Chapter 27

Visit to Missionaries in Taiwan

The journey to Taiwan by air is only a short one and there in Taipei, at the airport, were George and Frieda Foggin to meet me. Frieda is the daughter of my former fellow-worker in the school in Hinghwa, Mrs. Ruck, and she is the granddaughter of Mr. and Mrs. Hutton, our pioneer workers in that city. George is Canadian and had been working as a missionary in the Northwest of China for some years before I first met him, which meeting took place when he visited me in the German Hospital in Peking when my little daughter was born. When Frieda left Kuling where she had been teaching in the English boarding school to go to Peking where her father started a new Bible depot and evangelistic work, she met George, whom she married and they started missionary work together.

Theirs was a very nomadic life. Their children were each born in different parts of the world, by the Great Wall of China, in Portsmouth in England, in Rangoon in Burmah, in the far Northwest of China, in Peking and the last two in Taiwan, seven in all. After we were all obliged to leave China when the Communist regime took over completely, the Foggins started work in Taiwan and have continued there for more than twenty years. The last time I had seen them was in 1946 in the Willis home in Shanghai where we refugeed together for a few days before they flew off to Peking for the birth of their fifth child. So now we were able to enjoy a wonderful three weeks in their little house in the suburbs of Taipei, talking over all the old times and seeing the wonderful way in which God is still working out His plans. After the Second World War, Taiwan was freed from the Japanese who had ruled there for many years, and it later became the home of the Generalissimo Chiang Kai Shek and his wife with the Nationalist Army, forming the Republic of China.

It is a beautiful island, well supplied with good roads and railways by the former Japanese occupants. There is lovely coastal and mountain scenery, but also much fertile agricultural land. In the humid tropical climate, there are fine rice crops. The green paddy fields come right up to the border of the main roads. Fruit, too, is plentiful, peaches, apricots, mangoes, bananas and pineapple with other less known tropical fruits such as lichees. Moreover, there is now big industrial development. Much of the mission work is now done on the great trading estate among the hundreds of young factory workers.

Here in Taiwan I came back into my own, for Mandarin is the spoken language and it was a great joy to find that I had not forgotten it after all the years spent in England. What happy fellowship I enjoyed with all the members of their church in Peitou. Attached to the hall was a Christian kindergarten where over a hundred little Chinese children are collected each morning by coach to attend the classes held by devoted Chinese Christian teachers. How sweetly they sang to me the choruses and hymns they had learned and what a happy Chinese meal I was able to share with the staff one Saturday morning when George and Frieda spend time each weekend for prayer and Bible study with their helpers. At 6 a.m. each day, George is up to go to the hall to have a prayer session with the leading church members and on Sunday morning Frieda starts Sunday School at 8 a.m. after which other services follow in succession for most of the day. Meanwhile the home is open to visitors at all times, one never knew how many would be there to meals.

One incident of the love of their dear Chinese friends must be related. One day we had a visit from a Chinese brother who expressed great astonishment at the fact that, at my honourable age of 75, I was able to travel alone so far round the world, whereas most of their elderly ladies sit down and fold their hands at 60 years. The next morning at about 7 a.m. before I was fully dressed, he appeared at the door with a large basket of oranges to give me extra vitamins, I suppose. A few days later he came again with a black chicken. Now the Chinese think that a black-skinned chicken contains special nourishing powers and they give them as a present to convalescents or ladies who have just had a baby. When I asked Frieda if this dear man could really afford to make me such gifts, she replied, 'No, he is only a poor man but he feels that he has no gift for speaking for the Lord so he expresses his love in such ways.' To me this only added value to the presents and I am sure that the oranges and the black chicken will appear one day in the records kept by the Lord.

Three-Day Prayer Retreat

At the end of the second week, George drove us in the car up into the mountains to a beautiful camping ground, where a three-day prayer retreat for ladies was to be held. We each had small separate rooms in chalets with verandahs, so quiet and restful. Prayer was arranged in little groups in different parts of the compound, while the main meetings were held in a fine hall in the centre. Meals were in Chinese-style with chopsticks. There were delegates from all over Taiwan and there I met many of the old missionaries from China. We had stirring addresses by leading speakers, among whom was Mrs. Mitchell of the Youth for Christ in America. She herself had been a missionary in India and her husband has had much to do with the great revival in Sumatra. Another, who gave us a message, was Mrs. Dickeson, the organiser of 'Mustard Seed,' the splendid work for children in Taiwan, the helper of those in trouble with the authorities and the medical and midwifery work among the tribespeople in the mountainous district. One came away with an enlarged vision, realising that the small circle of work for God in which one usually moves is only a fraction of the work of the Holy Spirit in this world.

Encouraged by the Generalissimo and his wife, Christian missionaries are training the young people of East Asia that they may evangelise their own people in a day to come. At the home of Dr. and Mrs. West I met Dr. James Graham, the head of a big Bible school in Taipei and it was a thrill when he came up to me and asked whether I was the wife of Wilhelm or Gustav Koll. I found that he was one who, as a young missionary, had visited our mission station many years before.

At the dinner table, he told a story of an encounter he had had in the town of Saopao, one of the towns on the canal through which we had to pass on our way down to Shanghai. The steam launch on which he should have proceeded on his journey had been delayed, so he was held up there probably for many hours. At first he felt annoyed at the delay, but then the Lord reminded him that there is always a purpose in delays, so he started down the main street, visiting each shop with a tract. Then he caught a glimpse of an old priest sitting at the gate of the temple. He went over and had a chat with him and found that he was over eighty years old and rather sad about what would come when he was called away from this world. This was an opportunity to tell him of the love of God and His way of salvation and the old man listened with tears in his eyes. He had never heard anything so wonderful, but then he turned to the missionary and said, 'Why did you not come and tell me this before?'

Travelling in Taiwan

During the next week of my stay in Taiwan, Frieda took me to Tai-Chung, the important town in the centre of the island. We travelled by rail and I can only praise the standard of their railways, spotlessly clean carriages, nice curtains at the windows, a choice of teabags brought round by a steward, a continual supply of boiling water to make the tea in covered glasses, all at a minimal cost. On the return journey when we had to make an early start, we were supplied with a plastic container holding a roll, a banana and a biscuit for our breakfast with no extra cost above the ordinary rail ticket. We stayed with Miss Flanagan, a former missionary in Manchuria, in a charming little Japanese-style house, where all the partition walls were only sliding papered screens. One of her stories is a good illustration of what it sometimes means to live by faith.

When she arrived in Taiwan with some friends just after the war, they found a rather derelict house where they could live, so much so that, when they put the baby to sleep on a shelf, it rolled off on to the floor which collapsed and landed the child in a pool of water which lay underneath the boards. Moreover, they had scarcely any money left after renting the place. When they collected up the few pence left between them, the father went out and bought some spinach which with the remaining milk powder would provide a meal for the baby, but for themselves there was nothing left. Presently a Chinese friend, who had heard of their arrival, sent a message that he would call round to see them that evening. They did not try to put him off due to the meagre chance of showing hospitality, but left it in God's hands. Having tidied up the best they could, they awaited the guest, who arrived quite expecting to share the evening meal with them. After much polite and friendly conversation and yet no appearance of supper, he began to be suspicious, and took an opportunity to peep into the kitchen and realised that there was no preparation going on. He courteously withdrew, but not long afterwards they heard a knock at the door, and found the friend and his wife bringing along a hot cooked meal which she prepared at her home. 'Your Heavenly Father knoweth that ye have need of these things.'

While we were in Tai-Chung, we were able to have supper with two young missionaries we knew in England, Mary Thurlow and Barbara North, both of whom were doing language study at the time. A midday meal we shared with Mr. and Mrs. Conrad Bhaer, who have a very nice Bible bookshop on one of the main streets. They had been in Shanghai at the time we were refugeeing there in 1946 and did work in the Youth for Christ, to which meetings our own children were able to go. One evening they took us to the house of a Chinese lady where I was asked to give a message to a group of her neighbours. The next day we went to see the polio clinic run by Dr. and Mrs. Nicholls where they take apparently hopeless cases, caring for these children until they are fit to earn their own living or take their place in normal life.

Since Taiwan has freedom of religion, the Buddhists also make great efforts. On the outskirts of the city is a huge new statue of Buddha set on the crown of a hill — so big that one can climb up inside to look out of the eyes. Mrs. Nicholls also took us to see the temple of the Eighteen Hells. The Buddhists believe that when we leave this life, we go through all the hells to be punished for what we have done here. In China I have seen the small models of these tortures in small wooden cages placed at the entrance to the temples. In the temple at 'White Foal' village, our out-station, there was one containing a model of Mr. Hutton, our pioneer missionary, being trampled under the feet of a hideous looking devil, who is holding aloft a model of a torn Bible which the missionary had sought to teach. But here in Tai-Chung, the Eighteen Hells consists of life-size figures, being tortured, and they are animated mechanically. At the end of the cage sits the awful figure of the judge and, the most sad thing of all, is to see Chinese men and women, and even little children, watching the display and kneeling down to offer incense to the judge in the hope of being shown mercy when they die.

Outside, on the steps of the temple, was a little girl completely crippled with polio, crawling on her stomach up and down the steps begging. She had a sweet smiling face but Mrs. Nicholls would not give her money, but bought her cakes and ice cream instead. Then she told us privately the reason. Dr. and Mrs. Nicholls had rescued the child and had taken her to their clinic for treatment, but the next day the parents had changed their minds and had come to claim her back, not wishing her to be cured because she could earn more money for them with her sweet smile and crooked body.

Chapter 28

To the Missionary Conference in Jamaica

After three very happy weeks spent with these dear friends in Taiwan, the journey continued by plane to Los Angeles in California. Here on this trip another big wave arose as I suddenly realised that I should have had a visa for America in order to spend the night there. I was not due to arrive until 9:30 p.m. and was due to leave by plane for Jamaica the next morning at 8:30 a.m., so I had been under the impression that no visa would be required for such a short stay. At first I was anxious, but again committed it to the One who had said 'Come.' The problem had to be faced before we arrived in America.

Held Up at the Gateway

In Honolulu, Hawaii, we were all turned out of the plane with all the luggage to go through Customs and Passport Control. Apparently Honolulu is now the gateway to America.

When faced with the exclamation, 'You have no visa for America,' I tried to explain that I had not realised that it was necessary for a few hours, but suggested that I was willing to remain on the airport all night. This, however, would not be allowed, but I was told that I could spend the night with my friends in Montebello but that my travel ticket would be taken from me and would be returned to me when I left the States.

Mr. and Mrs. Will Missen were at Los Angeles airport to meet me and it was very nice to get to know them and get a glimpse of the publishing house* although the time was very short. The next morning we all set off together, also Gordon Bennett, who has now taken over the publishing house,† for we were all to travel on the Delta plane to Jamaica. The U. S. authorities were very courteous but they would not give me my ticket back until I was about to step into the plane. As the Delta plane had to fly over Cuba where there had been several hijacks during the previous weeks, we were all disembarked again in New Orleans, examined, frisked and searched, but all was well and we could continue our trip to Montego Bay in Jamaica, to arrive by 9:30 p.m., where we were met by friends from Oceanview Bible Camp where the Missionary Conference was to take place. At New Orleans, we had been joined by Mr. E. C. Hadley and his son, Samuel from Danville, Illinois, U.S.A., and Mr. W. A. Lickley from Australia.

The trip by car and minibus up to the camp took three or four hours. I shared a dormitory with Miss Harrow from Puerto Rico, Mrs. Dawson from New Zealand, Mrs. Davis from St. Kitts and Miss Regina Pearson and her sister from Philadelphia. Regina was formerly in charge of the girls' school in Mallawi in Egypt. It was a joyous reunion after so many years. There were missionaries from Colombia, the de Ruiters, the Rothlisbergers, Peter Nunn, the Poehners and Elsa Barolin who is head of the schools there. From Guyana were Luc Favarger and also Pierre Conod from Zurich,‡

---

* *Good Tidings Publishers, Inc.*

† *From 1973-1976. Now operates Overcomer Press, Inc., in Owosso, Michigan. G.T.P. is now located in St. Louis, Missouri, and managed by Mr. Lee Baseler.*

‡ *Now in missionary work in Quebec, Canada and St. Vincent respectively.*

who had just arrived on his way to take up work in Georgetown. From Europe came friends of long standing, Mr. Cuendet from Vevey, Mr. Georges André from Lausanne, Mr. and Mrs. Fred Pettman from England, while from the U.S.A. was my old friend Mr. Kaschel and many others whom I now can count in close circle.

From Oceanview to Eastbourne

The camp itself is beautifully situated, with a full view of the ocean and sea coast, with a swimming pool, park-like grounds and a lovely little chapel where we spent never-to-be-forgotten hours of praise, worship, and discussion about all the needs of missionary work. Much of the pleasure we owe to the care of dear Mr. and Mrs. A. Miller, and their helpers, who are in charge of the campsite.

It was a week of wonderful fellowship and renewal of interest in the Lord's work all over the world, the crowning point of my marvellous trip round the world, where the Lord held my hand and kept me from sinking all the way back via New York, and in the Jumbo Jet which carried me safely to Heathrow Airport, soon to be back in my little home in Eastbourne. One can only conclude the whole story by saying, 'Nought had failed of all that the Lord had promised.'

Epilogue
By Ruth Reveley

Elsie Koll returned from her long tour abroad in June, 1972, and spent the next four years in happy fellowship with the Christians meeting at Bourne Hall in Eastbourne, Sussex. Her time was happily occupied with visiting, speaking at women's meetings both in London and on the South Coast, and in showing hospitality to many of the Lord's people. Each autumn she enjoyed her visit to the Zurich Conference where she regularly interpreted the German 'talks' for the English visitors.

She was also engaged in translating daily readings from German into English for several years for a calendar printed by the German brethren.

In November, 1976, she came up to London to stay with her family for the celebration of her 80th birthday.

Almost immediately after this, she fulfilled a lifelong hope by visiting Helene Voorhoeve in Egypt, where she was able to have fellowship with the Lord's work amongst the young people in the schools there. An article on this visit was published in the missionary magazine LOOK September, 1977.*

LOOK, Sept./Oct., 1977, page 14, and republished in the following chapter.

While on holiday in Lynton, North Devon in June, 1977, she suffered a severe chill and bronchitis, and was not fully restored to health for some time. On September 8th, 1977, the family saw her off at Heathrow on her way to the Zurich Conference where she was to stay with her friends, the Gschwinds. While translating during the conference on the Saturday, Elsie Koll suffered a severe coronary and was in the intensive care unit of the Zurich hospital. The kindness of everyone, especially the Gschwinds, was heartwarming.

At last, with the full permission of her doctors, Elsie Koll was flown home to England on 28th September, her son, Godfrey, having gone to Switzerland to bring her home. She went to her daughter's home in Pinner where she died peacefully in her sleep three days later on the 1st October, 1977. In the Daily Light which she had read just before going to bed the night she went to be with the Lord were the following words, 'Thou wilt show me the paths of life . . . (with the Golden Thread running through it) and in Thy Presence is fulness of joy!'

Appendix

'I Wish
I Was
20 Years Younger'*
By Elsie Koll

A t the end of last year (1976) I had the great privilege
of making a visit to Egypt to visit my dear friend
Heleen Voorhoeve and have a personal look at her fine
work where she has served the Lord for nearly forty
years.

On arrival at Cairo Airport I was met by Mr. Fahmy,
his wife and their son who kindly took me to their home
for a few days. I was taken to see the Pyramids of
ancient Egypt. But more important, I met some of our
brethren in Cairo and saw the new conference hall
which seats 5,000 people which has a gallery that can
seat 500 more and a specially built alcove off the main
platform where translation can be made unseen by the
main audience.

Republished from LOOK Missionary Magazine.

The train journey up the Nile valley to Tema lasts about 6-7 hours, but was very pleasant with the densely cultivated fields on either bank and the sailing ships passing up and down the river.

During the train journey a young man seated in the opposite compartment approached me after much hesitation and said, "Are you going to see Miss Heleen?" He must have seen my luggage labels. I was surprised as I had refrained from attempting to converse with anyone as I could not speak Arabic and a woman travelling alone in a foreign country! When I replied in the affirmative he said, "Would you ask her to pray for my father who is very ill in Alexandria." I asked him to write down his name and tried to find out whether he was a Christian but the response was vague. Later Heleen told me neither his father nor he were Christians but they knew her and knew that she prayed.

Late in the evening Heleen met me with a horse carriage which they always hired, a rather shabby old victorian style vehicle, and we were soon at home in Bethel School.

800 Pupils

Bethel School has more than 800 pupils and it opens each morning with prayers and Bible reading conducted by the Headmistress in the school hall for all except the Mohammedan children. Then comes general assembly in the school playground for everyone where they sing and do physical exercises accompanied by the piano accordian played on the balcony by Heleen. What is most striking is the marvellous discipline — all these children in school uniform lined up in rank and order with no noise!

Lessons are from 8:30 a.m. to 1 p.m. and the teachers are all dear Egyptian Christians with whom I was able to have fellowship because several of them could speak good English. It takes some time to visit all the classrooms including a special kitchen for housewifery, a needlework room with several sewing machines and a geography room.

One of the great interests is on the roof where all the bread is baked in huge clay ovens fired by the garbage collected from the home where the teachers and boarders are housed. These also heat the bath water. The school maintains pigeon houses for hundreds of birds used chiefly as a source of meat. Chicken pens are divided up for laying hens, hatching birds and baby chickens. Then there are the two pig-sties, one with a big black sow and her eight piglets and the other with a boar. On the roof too is the laundry and the store-houses for rationed supplies of flour, rice, and beans. As one gazes from the roof over the whole town one realizes that most of the domestic chores are done on the roof! It seldom rains so everything is dry in a few minutes.

Splendid Outreach Work

The most wonderful experience for me was to see the splendid out-reach work. Most of you will have read of the two Halls of Peace and Light. There are no frills or attractions; only long wooden planks resting on pillars filled with cement which can be moved and arranged according to the need.

All the local High Schools including the Government Schools of Commerce and Technology finish at 1 p.m. Then the young students come voluntarily for a Bible lesson in Bethel. My first meeting was with 270 young girls, aged 15-20 years. After they were all seated Heleen sent for me and as I walked up the aisle past these rows and rows of teenagers I felt awed by a sense of responsibility for the message. I had brought my Chinese gospel posters with me to Egypt and I had a splendid interpreter, in Vittoria, one of the Egyptian teachers.

Again it was the silence which impressed me. After hymn-singing and prayer one could give the message to keen listeners and expect no interruption. After the meeting the teacher began to call the register of about 300 names, and as each one answered 'present' she got up and walked quickly out so that by the time that the last name was called the hall was empty without any confusion. On another occasion it was a group of senior boy students.

In the middle of the week was the Tabitha or Dorcas meeting — rows and rows of older ladies in their long black gowns which are drawn over the head and then fall like a cloak. There were a sprinkling of younger ladies too in bright coloured modern jerseys. About 250 attended — mostly mothers of the Bethel School children and all from the village.

On the Sunday I went with Heleen to the meeting in the assembly Meeting Room for the Breaking of Bread. After this they have a ministry meeting especially for the sisters who cannot usually get out to the weeknight meetings. This is held every evening at 5 o'clock. We went out before this began and on the way home seemed to collect the whole street for Sunday School. Heleen asked me to speak to the main group sitting on mats on the floor of the main school hall. They were about 200 in number and again perfect quiet with a ready response if one asked questions. At the same time there were two other classes of about 150 being held in the other two Halls.

A Love-Feast and Speeches

One day I was invited to a meeting in the assembly hall where there were about 80 sisters gathered for prayer just before I left Tema. The whole assembly gathered in the school hall. Some of the school children sang in English and Arabic and made speeches. After a love-feast they gave me all kinds of Egyptian souvenirs. I had learned at least one phrase in Arabic so as to greet them all as they each wanted to shake hands at the end.

What a work for the Lord is done in that Bethel School and Home! Dear Heleen is the heart of it all and a mother to the whole Tema assembly. She is constantly entertaining visitors, visiting brothers, Embassy strangers, and casual hippies as she is the only foreigner in the town and she takes it all in her stride on the spur of the moment.

I could say so much more also of our visit to Mallawi, to the school where Miss Pearson used to work but space does not allow. We went by hired car and to my astonishment were accompanied by an assistant to the driver but when we reached the market streets of Mallawi I understood, for he had to get out and shove the camels, push the donkeys and clear the way through the wares of the street vendors before the car could proceed.

On my return to Cairo I again enjoyed the loving hospitality of the Fahmy family for three days before I flew home. There are 16 meetings in Cairo* so I didn't even touch the fringe! One evening I was asked to speak to the young sisters at one of their halls and it was a joy to see so many young people keen to hear God's Word. It lasted about two hours in all because after the meeting and light refreshment they asked many questions about my conversion and my call to China.

The whole trip gave me a new vision of mission possibilities and my only wish is that I were twenty years younger!

---

*Now, in 1981, there are 18 meetings in Cairo.